Boss Tweed's New York

Seymour J. Mandelbaum was born in Chicago and studied at Princeton University and Columbia University. He is now professor of city and regional planning and history at the University of Pennsylvania. His other books include *Community and Communications*.

BOSS TWEED'S NEW YORK

SEYMOUR J. MANDELBAUM

With a New Introduction by the Author

ELEPHANT PAPERBACKS
Ivan R. Dee, Publisher, Chicago

BOSS TWEED'S NEW YORK. Copyright © 1965 by John Wiley
& Sons, Inc. This book was originally published in 1965 and is
here reprinted by arrangement with the author.

First ELEPHANT PAPERBACK edition published 1990 by
Ivan R. Dee, Inc., 1332 North Halsted Street, Chicago 60622.
Manufactured in the United States of America.

Library of Congress Cataloging-in-Publication Data
Mandelbaum, Seymour J.
    Boss Tweed's New York / Seymour J. Mandelbaum with a new
preface by the author.
    Reprint. Originally published: New York: Wiley, 1965. (New
dimensions in history. Historical cities)
    Includes bibliographical references.
    ISBN 0-929587-20-0
    1. New York (N.Y.)—Politics and government—To 1898.
2. Tweed Ring. 3. Tweed, William Marcy, 1823–1878. I. Title.
II. Series: New dimensions in history. Historical cities.
    F128.47.M28   1990   89-23377

PREFACE TO THE 1990 EDITION

I wrote *Boss Tweed's New York* (hereafter, simply *Tweed*) twenty-five years ago; as I read it now, the words seem almost to belong to another person. In preparing this new paperback edition, I have corrected a few minor errors, but I have not tried to reclaim the book by substantially revising the text or more subtly reshaping its meaning with an "up-to-date" interpretation. I have tried, instead, to place myself in the position of a reader coming upon the work for the first time, without any claim to the privileges of authorship.

As a new reader, I am at once intrigued and disturbed by the "time" of the book. *Tweed* describes its world as past: pre-subway, pre-telephone, and (as the original preface describes it) "defiantly pre-progressive." The ways in which New Yorkers of the 1860s and 1870s understood one another, represented and controlled their environment, raised revenue, and managed public enterprises mark them (in *Tweed*) as participants in a political culture that lies on the other side of a great divide.

The conclusion of the book—as if to maintain that distance and firmly to bury that culture—warns against a seductive nostalgia for the intellectual simplifications and institutional designs of the "world of the nineteenth century." "Living as we do in an age of great bureaucratic organizations," it cautions, "we are frequently, and properly, concerned with preserving individual spontaneity and freedom against the weight of institutional coordinators. The decentralized market society of the nineteenth century may tempt us as an answer to our contemporary dilemmas."

Reading *Tweed* now, I am not so sure that we have left this culture behind. *Tweed*'s world seems immanent in the structure of urban politics in the United States and therefore always possible. Martin Shefter argues this position directly when he insists that New York City's flirtation with bankruptcy in the 1970s was characteristic of a political cycle embedded in the conception of U.S. cities as competitive firms: they must justify themselves both in polling booths and in capital markets. In this cycle, the periodic creation of a fiscal crisis allows elite groups to discipline democratic demands for public services. Shefter interprets the events of 1871 which figure prominently in *Tweed* within this framework. Public works, real estate promotion, and broadly shared policy payoffs were linked in the expansive phase which *Tweed* describes as the "moment of opportunity." Subsequently, bankers and bond holders manufactured a "crisis" leading to fiscal and social contraction before budgetary constraints were relaxed in a new round of "politics as usual" which responded to long-delayed demands for infrastructure investments, jobs, and services.[1]

There may be something faintly mystical in imagining *Tweed*'s New York as an immanent practice. I am, however, uncertain about *Tweed*'s time even when I forgo such fantasies and try simply to judge the difference between past and present and to locate shifts in the discursive frames within which New Yorkers imagined the city and acted politically.[2]

On one level, the frames described in *Tweed* are both familiar and contemporary, easily recognizable despite the nineteenth-century locutions. Consider two compelling characterizations of the ways of talking in contemporary U.S. cities: Paul Peterson's treatment of "city limits," and Stephen Elkin's conception of cities as "commercial republics."[3]

Peterson describes U.S. cities as open systems unable to control the movement of labor or capital, heavily dependent on locally generated revenues, and prohibited from printing money. Under these circumstances, city polities cannot for very long appear to redistribute income from rich to poor. The appearance of

1. Martin Shefter, *Political Crisis/Fiscal Crisis: The Collapse and Revival of New York City* (New York: Basic Books, 1985).

2. I have quite deliberately used the term "discursive frames" rather than Michel Foucault's "discursive formations," in order to avoid endorsing all of the intellectual apparatus of that more familiar term. See Michel Foucault, *The Archaeology of Knowledge and the Discourse on Language*, trans. by A. M. Sheridan Smith (New York: Pantheon Books, 1972).

3. Paul E. Peterson, *City Limits* (Chicago: University of Chicago Press, 1981), and Stephen P. Elkin, *City and Regime in the American Republic* (Chicago: University of Chicago Press, 1987).

redistribution will inhibit new capital investment and encourage capital flight. Rather than redistribution, however just, strong competitive incentives encourage municipal officials to portray their choices as serving the "city as a whole." Policy discussions are crafted within this frame: participants argue over the definition of limits, the design of appearances, the collective meaning of distributional choices, and the distributional meaning of alternative ways of defining the common good.

Elkin, in contrast, describes a normative frame, a way that people *should* but only sometimes *do* talk when they engage the often conflicting implications of the idea that cities are both commercial corporations and republican polities; that they simultaneously seek to increase the wealth of their members and to cultivate and sustain the virtues, obligations, rights, and duties of citizenship.

The arguments spread across the pages of *Tweed* are embedded within these frames. Repeatedly they focus on the definition of limits, the nature of the collective good, the city as a corporation, and the claims of membership in the urban republic. Thus *Tweed's* world is part of our present.

On another level, however, *Tweed's* world seems not quite contemporary. The passion with which these matters were addressed in the 1860s and 1870s is a clue that we are in a foreign land. Cities cannot be morally obligated to act beyond their limits. In our time, however, defining those limits (however contentious) is always rhetorically tied to a conception of the responsibilities of state and national governments: they must do what cities cannot! The "safety net"—particularly in the depression of the 1870s—seemed so vital an urban issue in *Tweed's* New York, and the implications of "limits" so devastating, because of the fiscal and institutional weaknesses of other governments.[4] The poor had to fight in "city

4. Stephen Skowronek, *Building a New American State: The Expansion of National Administrative Capacities, 1877–1920* (Cambridge, England: Cambridge University Press, 1982); C. K. Yearley, *The Money Machines: The Breakdown and Reform of Governmental and Party Finances in the North, 1860–1920* (Albany: State University of New York, 1970); Kenneth Fox, *Better City Government: Innovation in American Urban Politics, 1850–1937* (Philadelphia: Temple University Press, 1977); and L. Ray Gunn, *The Decline of Authority: Public Economic Policy and Political Development in New York State, 1800–1860* (Ithaca: Cornell University Press, 1988).

trenches" within the discursive frame of "city limits" because the alternatives were so meager.[5]

Had I written this new preface in the 1970s, the weakness of the federal presence in *Tweed*'s world would have been the surest sign of its remoteness. Theodore Lowi argued in 1979, for example, that the rapid increase in intergovernmental transfer payments and the links between city halls and Washington that had been forged since the 1960s had created a new constitutional order, a "Second Republic."[6] *Tweed* belonged to the First Republic that had passed.

Subjective time is not constructed along a straight arrow but moves back and forth from past to future across a shifting landscape.[7] While the decline of the "intergovernmental city,"[8] beginning in the last years of the Carter administration, has by no measure restored the federal system of the First Republic, it surely has reduced the distance that separates us from *Tweed*. The federal urban presence of the 1960s and 1970s is now part of our past that appears (like *Tweed*) as a cautionary memory or an aspiration.[9]

Conflicts between the commercial and the republican aspects of city polities in the 1870s also seem rawer and more passionate than our current sensibilities lead us to expect. Why, I wondered

5. Antonio Gramsci argued that "the superstructures of civil society are like the trench-systems of modern warfare." Ira Katznelson, *City Trenches: Urban Politics and the Patterning of Class in the United States* (New York: Pantheon Books, 1981) has elaborated this notion in a study of the impact of municipal autonomy and the politics of neighborhood on the articulation of class conflict. For a critical exchange on this matter, see Terrence J. McDonald, "The Burdens of Urban History: The Theory of the State in Recent American Social History," *Studies in American Political Development: An Annual*, 3 (1989), 3–29, followed by a comment by Ira Katznelson and a reply by McDonald, 30–55.

6. Theodore J. Lowi, "The State of Cities in the Second Republic," in John P. Blair and David Nachmias, ed., *Fiscal Retrenchment and Urban Policy*. Urban Affairs Annual Reviews, 17 (Beverly Hills, Calif.: Sage Publications, 1979), 43–54.

7. I have elaborated these notions in "Temporal Conventions in Policy Discourse," *Environment and Planning B: Planning and Design*, 11 (1984), 5–13.

8. Robert W. Burchell *et al.*, *The New Reality of Municipal Finance: The Rise and Fall of the Intergovernmental City* (New Brunswick, N.J.: Center for Urban Policy Research, 1984).

9. Charles Murray, *Losing Ground: American Social Policy, 1850–1980* (New York: Basic Books, 1984); John Mollenkopf, *The Contested City* (Princeton: Princeton University Press, 1983); and Mark Gottdiener, *The Decline of Urban Politics: Political Theory and the Crisis of the Local State*. Sage Library of Social Research, 162 (Newbury Park, Calif: Sage Publications, 1987).

as I read the account of the Tilden Commission in Chapter 15, were elite groups so apprehensive? Didn't they understand the banality of city politics, the ease with which it could be controlled, and the variety of sanctuaries to which they had ample access?[10]

My questions are signs leading to a difference. The elites then did not understand what, after all, largely lay in the future. *Tweed* or Amy Bridges' account of the "origins of machine politics" in antebellum New York describe the development of political institutions which were neither hierarchical nor tightly disciplined but rather were robust and served remarkably to contain social conflict.[11] Only at the turn of the century did economic and social elites fully grasp the security of a stable and disciplined city-wide party organization.[12]

The sanctuaries were also fewer. The advantages of Manhattan as a site of residence were probably greater in *Tweed's* New York than they have been at any time since the opening of the Brooklyn Bridge in 1883. Yet the common ground was already socially differentiated by 1870, and the salience of land use change encouraged a sense of imminent danger even in the best neighborhoods.

The external sanctuaries were also fewer than in our own day. *Tweed* presents the Tilden Commission's report as if it were a reactionary throwback to the era of the chartered city corporation.[13] I read it now in quite a different way. The commission was still engaged by the emergent judicial distinction between publicly chartered "private" corporations and "public" cities with coercive powers but limited authority.[14] While the restrictive program advocated by the commission clearly failed (in New York and

10. That is the retrospective wisdom expressed in Terrence J. McDonald, *The Parameters of Urban Fiscal Policy: Socioeconomic Change and Political Culture in San Francisco, 1860–1906* (Berkeley: University of California Press, 1986).

11. Amy Bridges, *A City in the Republic: Antebellum New York and the Origins of Machine Politics* (Ithaca: Cornell University Press, 1984).

12. David C. Hammack, *Power and Society: Greater New York at the Turn of the Century* (New York: Russell Sage Foundation, 1982).

13. Hendrik Hartog, *Public Property and Private Power: The Corporation of the City of New York in American Law, 1730–1870* (Chapel Hill: University of North Carolina Press, 1983).

14. Gerald Frug, "The Legal Concept of the City," *Harvard Law Review*, 93 (1980), 1057–1153; and Robert C. Ellickson, "Cities and Homeowners Associations," *University of Pennsylvania Law Review*, 130 (1982), 1519–1580, with comments by Frank I. Michelman and Frug and a reply by Ellickson, 1581–1608.

elsewhere) to structure city governance, it did sustain the multiplication of suburbs and homeowners associations[15] in which its defensive strategies could be implemented. We have become so accustomed to a world in which these sanctuaries are ubiquitous that we are easily surprised by apprehensions of "commercial republics" in a (distant) world in which there was very little protected space.

What of communication? I have argued to this point that the discursive frames of politics in Tweed's world were close to our own, but that they were invested with an unfamiliar passion and meaning rooted in the dynamics of the federal system more than a century ago and in the unrelieved intensity of conflict over common urban ground.

That, of course, is not the argument of the book itself. Tweed describes its world as distant because it precedes a great communications revolution which allowed "us" to enrich our shared sense of community and our capacities for both collective and cooperative action. 1870 is different from 1965 (and, presumably, from 1990) because over the century, urban polities were progressively enabled to imagine, execute, and control development projects, to shape their environments, and to know themselves and what they had done.

Tweed is saved—at least in my reading—from being trivially optimistic about "progress" because it does not assume that "reformers" spoke with the voice of the future, that either cash or policy payoffs precluded competence, that tacit knowledge was equivalent to ignorance, or that the conventional categories of political debate in the 1860s and 1870s accurately described behavior.[16]

The sophistication of the account does not, of course, establish its validity. Is it true that our capacities for collective and cooperative action and intelligent city-building have increased over the last

15. Ellickson, "Cities and Homeowners Associations," and Jon C. Teaford, *City and Suburb: The Political Fragmentation of Metropolitan America, 1850–1970* (Baltimore: Johns Hopkins University Press, 1979).

16. Jon Teaford, *The Unheralded Triumph: City Government in America, 1870–1900* (Baltimore: Johns Hopkins University Press, 1984), and McDonald, *The Parameters,* have (wrongly, in my view) indicted a generation of urban political historians for these sins.

century? If there has been such an increase, did it depend critically on a transformation in communication?

These are hard questions, and I am no longer sure they are phrased in a way that allows them to be answered cogently. The conception of communication in *Tweed* is very catholic—or, some might say, impossibly ambiguous. Under the communication umbrella are matters as diverse as the number and range of clubs for women, the rhetoric and circulation of newspapers, the reliability of mail delivery, and the inadequacies of government fiscal accounts and measures of unemployment. The analyses of corruption, leadership, and decentralization relate institutional arrangements to the flow of information as if organization and communication were distinct. Institutions are also, however, interpreted as communication networks—a decentralized political machine is like a telephone system in which local calls are cheap while long-distance connections are difficult or expensive—so that it is very difficult to distinguish dependent and independent variables.

The claim of increasing intelligence and public competence is also suspect. At a project scale—sewers, tunnels, high-rise buildings, subways, street pavements, water treatment plants—it is hard to resist the conventional notion that both social and technological "knowhow" have increased the range and effectiveness of collective action. At a larger system scale, however, it is not similarly clear that we have grown more competent. Competence seems to generate an overreaching ambition that dooms us to frustration. Aware of our flaw, we are prone to write the history of regional or environmental planning in the narrative forms appropriate to tragedies.[17] The development of communications has impoverished some communities and enriched others. It is difficult as an analyst to describe the dynamics of that balance or (what has come to interest me more) as a planner to use the new media to shape an intense urban citizenship.[18]

Tweed may well be ambiguous, confused, naive, or even dead

17. Peter Hall, *Cities of Tomorrow: An Intellectual History of Urban Planning and Design in the Twentieth Century* (Oxford, England: Basil Blackwell, 1988).

18. *Community and Communications* (New York: W. W. Norton, 1972) and "Cities and Communication: The Limits of Community," in Joel A. Tarr and Gabriel Dupuy, ed., *Technology and the Rise of the Network City in Europe and America* (Philadelphia: Temple University Press, 1988), 309–321.

wrong on some of these matters. That troubles me very little. In everything that I have written post-*Tweed* I have refined its terms, played against its arguments, or found myself proposing *Tweed*-like ideas in strange settings. Its difficulties have been productive for me, and I am delighted that they are now again accessible to a new generation of readers.

S.J.M.

Philadelphia, Pennsylvania
January 1990

PREFACE

During the nineteenth century, society in the United States was fundamentally democratized. Men announced themselves "equal," and cast off many of the remaining bonds of both an inherited social hierarchy and limiting tradition. The power to make significant decisions was widely diffused to competing elites and to individuals. Institutions that had controlled and stabilized life were caught in the flood of rapid change and abandoned their older functions.

Boss Tweed's New York is part of a growing body of literature that breaks with the assumption of older liberal historians who praised the people, complained when popular power was limited and moaned only occasionally about the aberrations of the majority will. I view the "faults" of the nineteenth century—the cruelty of slavery, the terror of the Civil War, the denuded forests and the exciting but also hellish cities—in another light. They seem to me to have been intrinsic parts of the democratization of American society. Blessings and curses were intertwined in a process that was both enormously liberating and profoundly tragic.

Many analytical models, many points of view, have been brought to bear in the attempt to understand the dynamics of a society in transition. Historians and sociologists have suggested that the distribution of values, of income, of social respect, or of power provide clues to the most general patterns of social behavior. This study of politics in New York City in the 1860's and 1870's complements these suggestions with a communications model of man and society. Men are organisms linked together by a network through which messages are carried. The manner in which they make decisions is critically affected by the information at their disposal and their ability to use it.

Boss Tweed's New York is then, to put it somewhat too simply, a study in the distribution of information. Tweed himself is a symbol of a society with a primitive communications network. The problems of New York a century ago were no less complex than those of a twentieth century metropolis of comparable size. Its communications network could not, however, link the several parts of the city together. The techniques of the era for gathering and analyzing information could not cope with the complexity of its problems. As a result, difficult issues took on a forced simplicity, in spite of themselves and at great cost. Rigid social stereotypes were perpetuated and political decisions were forced into the market place.

The focus on communication and information will, I hope, interest readers whose normal concerns are quite apart from those usually defined in American political history. Across the world, anxious men are asking questions about the appropriate balance between private and public planning, between democracy and autocracy, between "good" government and popular government. Many of them believe that the capacity of their communications network and their information systems critically shape the manner in which this balance is struck. I would like to think that readers in New Delhi and Rio de Janeiro may find some common ground with the inhabitants of Boss Tweed's New York.

Several years ago, I thought of writing a book on the longing for community among American intellectuals. I described this longing as a "nostalgia," or what Morton Grodzins calls a "gemeinschaft grouse." This study of New York politics reflects a profound change of mind. Men, it seems to me, flourish in communities where they face each other in a common discourse about values and goals, and in which they believe that it is possible to act as a community.

This book is not, however, about the individual feeling of belonging or alienation. Many readers will miss an extended discussion of the psychological stress of immigration, the culture of poverty or the loneliness of even the new native urbanite. The stress in these pages is upon the total institutional impact— and particularly, the political impact—of these profound individual experiences.

The decision to study New York in the late 1860's and 1870's stemmed in part from a conviction that American historians had confused the study of change and the study of reform. I hope that this book offers some useful distinctions since Boss Tweed's New York had the advantage of being defiantly pre-progressive. It should be clear, however, that my moral purposes are insistently reformist. The empirical statements that appear in these pages will, I hope, prove acceptable and valuable to men of diverse values. The social criticism which is apparent in many of these statements is intended for the present and for the future city in which our children will live. Lecturing the present with the example of the past—if the past is not distorted—is one of the noblest functions of the historian's craft.

There is one important financial debt on my ledger. I have several times received assistance from the Professional Development Fund of the Division of Humanities and Social Sciences, Carnegie Institute of Technology. I owe many intellectual debts, some of which are acknowledged in the following pages. Two of these debts are so great that they are written on every page. Professor Robert A. Lively of Princeton University saw this work through its most difficult graduate school days. My wife, Dorothy Rosenthal Mandelbaum, taught me to be sensitive to the problems of human communication. Her insights preceded and infused with meaning all of the more formal theoretical statements that appear in the text. More than she will allow, she is the co-author of this book.

SEYMOUR J. MANDELBAUM

Pittsburgh, Pennsylvania
December, 1964

CONTENTS

LIST OF ILLUSTRATIONS

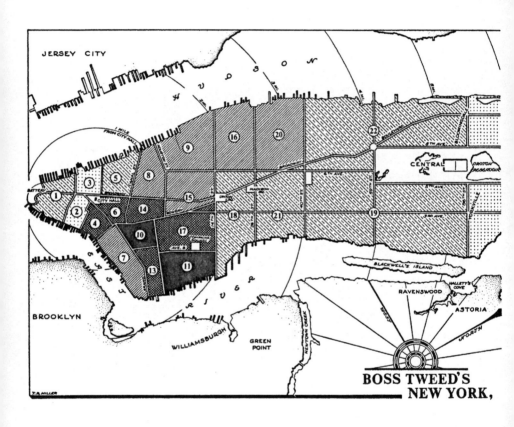

BOSS TWEED'S
NEW YORK,

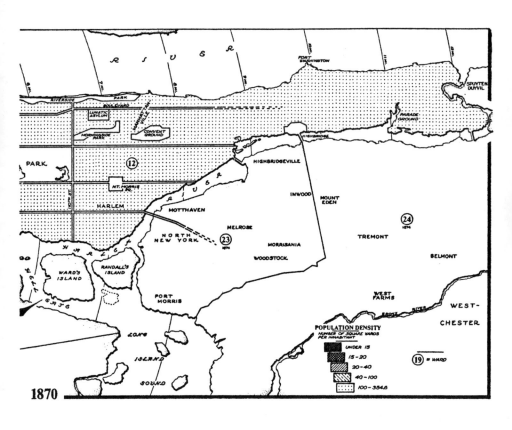

1870

POPULATION DENSITY
NUMBER OF SQUARE YARDS
PER INHABITANT

- UNDER 15
- 15-20
- 20-40
- 40-100
- 100-354.8

(19) = WARD

ONE

Communication and Community

Daily during the 1850's—"and many a time since," he wrote in 1881—Walt Whitman gazed across New York harbor from the deck of the Fulton Street Ferry, crossing between the still separate cities of Brooklyn and New York. Steam and sail and ocean current connected the metropolis to the world and engulfed the poet in their wonder and their vitality. The ferry sights merged in his imagination with his vision of the city. Men and water were caught in an evershifting, throbbing movement. Returning to New York for his first extended visit after the long and weary war, he found the "daily contact and rapport with its myriad people, on the scale of the oceans and tides, the best, most effective medicine my soul has yet partaken."

Whitman loved New York, yet he judged it severely. The city, he cried, was still engaged in the great battle against a past which lauded order, safety, caste, authority, and cohesion. The revolutionary anger against the constraints of tradition was still raw, and constantly renewed, in 1870. Swelled with the hurts and the pride of battle, New York was a city of individuals cut off from each other. "We live," he pleaded, "in an atmosphere of hypocrisy throughout. The men believe not in the women, nor the women in the men. A scornful superciliousness rules in literature . . . Conversation is a mass of badinage." [1]

Whitman grappled with the problems which had worried the minds and tormented the hearts of Western men since the seventeenth century. Difficulties of communication (in large part, the

---

[1] Walt Whitman, "Specimen Days," and "Democratic Vistas," in Malcolm Cowley, ed., *Complete Poetry and Prose of Walt Whitman* (New York: Pellegrini and Cudahy, 1948), II, pp. 12, 115, 214, 216–218.

1

product of vastly expanded aspirations) appeared both as symptoms of change and as dynamic elements conditioning the course of development. These difficulties struck deep because they appeared in the inner sanctum of the family. There was a break in the accustomed transfer of values and information between generations. Parents and educational theorists in the seventeenth century had begun to insist upon the special characteristics and needs of the young. Words unfit for children were differentiated from the normal flow of adult conversation. The transmission of culture between generations more and more became the task of institutions removed from the mainstream of work-a-day life—the schools—with their own rules and language. Young and old communicated at a distance and through an intermediary.[2]

Each new generation caught up in the process of modernization experienced a sense of internal crisis as the lines of communication between young and old broke. Young men with a deep-felt need to achieve new goals could not listen to the hesitant voices of the old or of their peers who still clung to the ways of the past. "Resisting, rejecting, not giving in to the majority—that was their secret." [3] They reversed a centuries old order of values. The modernizers preferred profits and privacy to communion with familiar faces in a familiar setting. Parents who were not fully committed to the new age trained their children to be free to move and yet loyal to old ideals. They were, therefore, both fulfilled and frustrated by their offspring's successes. The children, for their part, sang of the sadness and the guilt of a parting which could not be avoided but which came too early.[4]

New York, a city of immigrants, was caught up in repeated crises of understanding and compassion which transcended the physical problems of the streets and the newspapers as media of communication. A manual for Irish immigrants published in the

[2] Bernard Bailyn, *Education in the Forming of American Society* (Chapel Hill: The University of North Carolina Press, 1960), pp. 21–26; Phillip Ariès, *Centuries of Childhood,* trans. Robert Baldick (New York: Knopf, 1962).
[3] The phrase is Consuelo Sanchez's. Oscar Lewis, *The Children of Sanchez, Autobiography of a Mexican Family* (New York: Random House, 1961), p. 424.
[4] Erik Erikson, *Childhood and Society* (New York: Norton, 1950), pp. 250–255.

seventies anxiously described the familial conflict inherent in the process of acculturation into the American way. It urged new migrants to work hard, study and save to get ahead. But, the author pleaded, "filial devotion" and "love of friends" are "characteristics of our race that deserve all honor." The same tension between achievement and the community plagued the Puritan colony in Massachusetts two centuries earlier. Church, commonwealth, and family, the Synod of 1679 moaned, are being destroyed by self-assertion.[5]

The destruction of the traditional family structure and of the pattern of close communal relations of which it was a part had a profound impact upon all of Western society. Political institutions could not contain the flood of newly significant voices. Kings and parliaments trembled. Municipal corporations lost control of their destinies. In a rigidly circumscribed way, men in a stable aristocratic society had understood one another. In the process of transition, as Alexis de Tocqueville noted in the 1830's, understanding vanished. Relations between masters and servants, citizens and rulers, were infected by a "secret and intestine warfare," which could only be stilled with the growth of a new and free democratic discourse.[6]

The impact of changes in the patterns of communication was apparent in the United States at the highest levels of national affairs. The strong central government created in the 1780's and early 1790's was based upon the close ties between members of small political elites. Contests between these elite members forced them to appeal directly to the electorate at home. Changes in the social structure of their districts also tended to drive the leaders closer to the views of their constituents. In the absence of broad national channels of mass communication, the democratization of politics drained power from the central capital.[7]

[5] The Rev. Stephen Byrne, O.S.D., *Irish Emigration to the United States* (New York, 1873), p. 73; Perry Miller, *The New England Mind: From Colony to Province* (Cambridge: Harvard University Press, 1953), pp. 33–38.
[6] Alexis de Tocqueville, *Democracy in America*, trans. Phillips Bradley (New York: Knopf, 1954), II, p. 195.
[7] This analysis is similar to that of William Nisbet Chambers, *Political Parties in a New Nation, The American Experience, 1776–1809* (New York: Oxford University Press, 1963).

This national experience was duplicated in countless public and private organizations. The essence of this experience may be captured in an abstract model.[8] Think of an organization as divided into two parts, a center for making decisions and several points of contact with the external environment which operate both as sources of information and agencies for action. When the flow of information from these points to the central decision-making body is weak or costly, they tend to assume responsibility for making decisions. The same effect occurs if the techniques of the central decision-makers for storing, selecting and analyzing information cannot keep up with the flood of messages which inundates them. In either case, decisions tend to be made at the edges rather than at the center of the organization. The ranchers, unable to reach the cavalry, take the law into their own hands. The central manager, unable to find out what is going on in the shops, allows the foremen to set piece rates and determine the work rules.

There is, however, a strong contrary tendency. When the decision center finds it difficult to transmit messages to the points of action, it attempts to do—and decide—as much as it can. The president insists on signing every paper himself. The political boss takes all of the important offices into his own hands. Equally as important, every attempt at central coordination takes on the appearance of autocracy in the eyes of the beneficiaries of decentralization. John Kelly, presiding gingerly over a weak New York City government in the 1870's, in reform speeches appeared to be "as absolute a dictator as was known in the history of Rome." [9]

The tension between apparent autocracy and decentralization pervaded nineteenth century life. Change was so rapid that it was impossible to find a stable point of equilibrium around which the distribution of power could fluctuate. Attempts to solve one communication problem stimulated changes in another area

[8] An abstract model does not, of course, tell the "whole truth" or represent a social situation in its vivid human detail. If it did, it would be neither abstract nor useful. The elements of the simple model presented here are drawn from Herbert A. Simon, *Administrative Behavior* (2nd. ed., New York: Macmillan, 1957) and James G. March and Herbert A. Simon, *Organizations* (New York: Wiley, 1959).

[9] Abram Hewitt, quoted in the *New York Tribune*, October 25, 1878.

and added to the chorus of voices. Formal political parties were organized to express opinions which could no longer be channeled through the eighteenth century networks of faction and family. The parties not only channeled opinions, they elicited them. Government officials, responsive to a multitude of conflicting demands, abandoned their claims to social leadership. Improvements in communications opened new business opportunities and stimulated vast movements of population across continents. Village and city, New York and County Cork, suddenly connected, flooded each other with men and ideas. Business firms, swollen in size, outgrew the capacity of their owners to control their operations. Cities outgrew the stride of man's two walking feet. A tight network of voluntary associations could no longer diffuse a sense of belonging and being "listened to." Workers, out of touch with their employers, their own families, and their urban environment called for a new brotherhood of free communion.

The difficulties of communication encouraged men to make decisions on their own. In a society of independent, individual decision-makers, the mechanisms of the market place, which gave every commodity and every man a price, dominated society. Individual decisions were cumulated in the market, resources were allocated, and the quality of life determined. The market knew only two criteria for choice: "How much will you pay?" and "How much do you want?" There appeared to be no other mechanism capable of making decisions on a more complex set of criteria. The alternative to decentralized market decision-making, men of good spirit believed, was an ignorant autocracy. Even humane acts of charity were suspect because they ignored the criteria of the marketplace. They threatened the insistence on individual responsibility in a society which could not collectively solve its own problems. Individuals had to be forced into the market place, where problems could be solved.[10]

The criteria of the market place infected almost every activity. Even Adam Smith had cautioned that public works, justice, and national defense required government initiative and planning.

[10] Karl Polanyi, *The Great Transformation, The Political and Economic Origins of Our Time* (New York: Farrar and Rinehart, 1944) is a pioneering examination of the role of the market place in nineteenth century society.

Walt Whitman, Civil War reporter, could testify to the difficulties of exempting these activities from the rule of price: justice was bought and sold, Congressmen were bribed to give away public lands, and profiteers fattened themselves on war contracts. Attempts to break from this pattern foundered on the limitations of the communications network. Abraham Lincoln, leading the nation in a time of deep crisis, held no press conferences and thought that public political addresses would demean his station. The press was almost necessarily given over to gossip and rumor.[11]

The tragedy of the war and the costs of the reign of the market lay heavily upon Walt Whitman as he returned to New York in the later sixties. He pleaded for a heightened responsiveness to communication and a class of master communicators to relieve the loneliness and the narrow materialism of American culture. The nation required a new "personalism," uniting a deep respect for individual dignity with a passion for humanity and comradeship. It required a new literary class to elevate and unify the community of free men.[12]

The process of social change is more pedestrian than Whitman imagined. The communications network which made it possible to coordinate, rather than simply to cumulate, decisions and to alter the market allocation of resources, was fashioned from paved streets, elevated lines, settlement houses, political clubs, cheap newspapers and standard administrative forms—and not from poems. The master communicators were less noble than Whitman had hoped. Nevertheless, the poet's fundamental insight captured the spirit of the city. New York in 1870—the American nation in 1870—was a democracy in the midst of a still incomplete communications revolution.

[11] David Donald, *Lincoln Reconsidered* (New York: Knopf, 1956), pp. 59–60.
[12] Whitman, *op. cit.*, pp. 209–213.

TWO

Benchmarks and Barriers

The population of New York at the close of the Civil War was a little less than a million. It is difficult, however, to tell just how much less. Counting the population of the city taxed the techniques and institutions of the sixties for gathering and reporting information. The returns of the state census of 1865 were tabulated by hand by a single clerk. No attempt was made to check his work. The census takers, who recorded only 726,386 inhabitants, were charged with manipulating their findings in order to reduce the city's legislative delegation. The United States Office of the Census was also charged with political bias in 1870 and President Grant was forced to order a recount. The Superintendent of the Census vigorously defended against attack the revised figure of 942,292. At the same time, he bitterly complained against the legal and technical difficulties which limited the accuracy of all his efforts.[1]

The suspicion which greeted every census and every estimate of the rate of unemployment, of crime or of school truancy had important implications for public policy in New York. It is difficult to plan for an inherently unknowable future. It is more difficult to plan when even the present is cloaked in mystery. For the moment, however, this suspicion is chiefly important as a warning: the measures we use to frame New York's proportions in our own mind's eye, are rough indeed.

[1] United States Bureau of the Census, *Ninth Census of the United States: 1870* (Washington, D. C., 1872), I, pp. xx-xxxviii. All the statistical data for 1870 in this and subsequent chapters is drawn from the national census. For the difficulties of counting, also see New York Secretary of State, *Census of the State of New York for 1875* (Albany, 1875), pp. vii-x, xxxiii-xxxiv.

New York was a varied city, impressing visitors with its multiple faces. It was a rich metropolis—the commercial, banking, and artistic capital of the American continent. It was also a poor city. The streets in most areas were dirty and improperly drained. The air in good sections and in bad (there was no way of barring the wind) stank with the exhalations of slaughter houses, gas works, decaying garbage, and the festering bodies of dead animals. The death rate in 1864 (40 in every 1000) was higher than that of any other large city in the Western world. The lower classes suffered from annoying and persistent physical illness and disability. The infant mortality rate in the tenements was twice that in the private dwellings.[2]

New York was a democratic city in which power was widely diffused to many competing elites. And yet, at the same time, the distribution of income was radically skewed to the two extremes. Persons of modest means were rare. The inhabitants, as economist Rufus Tucker argued, "were either rich or very poor, mainly the latter." [3]

New York was a city built on motion and on the hope of improvement. Forty-four per cent of the population in 1870 had been born abroad—21 per cent in Ireland, 16 per cent in the German states. Within the city, the immigrants (from across the seas and from nearby Massachusetts) engaged in a frenetic dance. "That's the way to live in New York—to move every three or four years," Arthur Townsend in Henry James' *Washington Square* explained. "Then you always get the last thing. It's because the city's growing so quick—you've got to keep up with it." [4]

Townsend was exhilarated by change. The city shouted its excitement. Others, in quieter and more desperate straits, moved wearily and without hope. A tenement, a newspaper reporter

[2] *Report of the Council of Hygiene and Public Health of the Citizens Association of New York Upon the Sanitary Condition of the City* (New York, 1865).
[3] Rufus Tucker, "The Distribution of Income Among Income Taxpayers in the United States, 1863–1935," *Quarterly Journal of Economics*, LIII (1938), pp. 563–566.
[4] Henry James, *Washington Square*, in William Phillips, ed. *Great American Short Novels*, (New York: Dial Press, 1946), p. 99.

commented, is like the steerage deck of a ship where men are thrown together, knowing that they will be soon parted.[5]

The political boundaries of New York in 1870 were still fixed around Manhattan and the small islands in the East River. The city was, however, the center of a great metropolitan region, sharing the advantages of the finest harbor and the most extensive market in the United States. The region was growing faster than the city itself. Brooklyn, with 400,000 inhabitants, was the third largest town in the United States. It had quadrupled its population between 1850 and 1870. Newark's rise from a city of 40,000 to one of 100,000 had been almost as rapid. Jersey City outdid them both. First listed as a separate town in 1840, the booming rail center boasted more than 80,000 citizens in 1870. The spaces between the urban nodes of the metropolitan region were dotted with suburban settlements. Businessmen submitted to the long trip each day from Westchester or New Jersey in order to enjoy "more space for health, pleasure and privacy," than the city afforded.[6]

The metropolitan region was the center of a great communications network stretching across the nation and across the world. The fortunes of the entire region were dependent upon the massive movement of men, money, and goods to and from its market places. New York businessmen looked to the federal government to ease this movement and to expand the flow of information which preceded the transport of materials. Trade with Latin America, Asia, and Africa, for example, was inhibited by uncertainties which stemmed at least in part from ignorance. American consuls there were few and far between, poorly paid, and poorly chosen. Their reports were published annually and were of very little use. During an appropriations debate in 1878, Congressman Abram Hewitt

[5] Quoted in the *Report of the Council of Hygiene and Public Health of the Citizens Association of New York Upon the Sanitary Condition of the City,* (New York, 1865), p. lxxx.
[6] The characteristics of the region are described in United States Bureau of the Census, *Tenth Census of the United States: 1880,* XVIII, "Report on the Social Statistics of Cities" (Washington, D. C., 1886) pp. 531–597. The desire for space is described by George H. Foster, an inhabitant of Westchester County, in a letter to Mayor Havemeyer, April 13, 1874, Mayors Papers, Box 223.

said that he was willing to sacrifice the European consulates, whose services were largely political, in favor of increased funds for commercial representatives in South and Central America.[7]

New Yorkers Hamilton Fish and William Evarts, as Secretaries of State in Washington, struggled to improve the consular service. First in 1871 and then in a series of general consular regulations in 1874, Fish demanded uniform reports and placed greater emphasis upon commercial information. Limited attempts were made to improve the character of the service. Evarts promised the New York Chamber of Commerce in 1877 that the consuls would act as "earnest co-operators with the industry of manufacturers and the zeal of commerce." He aroused the consuls to renewed efforts to promote trade and began to issue trade bulletins to the daily press. The first special reports published outside the annual volumes on commercial relations were issued in 1879.[8]

New Yorkers had more success with the federal government than they had within their own region. The institutions of what we now call the metropolitan area were not structured to coordinate the plans and politics of its separate though interdependent parts. The growth of Newark and Jersey City seemed to depend upon a continued gap in the transportation network which linked New York to the outside world. Only the lines of the New York Central system actually entered Manhattan. The other major trunk line railroads to the West and South were confined by the Hudson to the Jersey shore. They were forced to ferry cargo and passengers across the river. Jersey City, the major point of transfer, prospered. Congestion on the New York docks forced steamship companies,

[7] The *New York Tribune*, March 12, 1878. I have consistently chosen to cite the *New York Tribune*, which is available on microfilm in most libraries, in preference to other city papers, even the official *City Record*. This should simplify the task of readers who are engaged by a particular incident or statement and would like to look at the contemporary record for themselves. Where events are identified with a precise date and no reference is given, it can be presumed that an account appears in the next morning's *New York Tribune*.

[8] *Twentieth Annual Report of the Chamber of Commerce of the State of New York For the Year 1877–'78* (New York, 1878), p. 14; Eugene Schuyler, *American Diplomacy and the Furtherance of Commerce* (New York; Scribner's, 1886), pp. 32–34.

eager for a Manhattan location, to seek berths elsewhere. New Jersey's future seemed to lie in a competitive struggle for the advantages of the harbor, rather than in cooperative planning of the region's development.

Brooklyn was more tightly linked to New York than were the New Jersey towns. Brooklynites depended heavily upon the New York City papers for even their local news. Nine ferry boats carried more than 48,000,000 passengers across the East River in 1868. The severe winter of 1866–1867 emphasized the uncertainties of the water connection and stimulated planning for a permanent bridge.[9] The state legislature in Albany provided a common meeting ground for the representatives of the two cities. In the decade after 1857, the legislature created metropolitan boards of police, fire, health, and excise with jurisdiction over Brooklyn, New York, and adjoining areas in Westchester, Richmond, and Queens. The metropolitan boards gained administrative strength from their independence of the local political structures in each of the cities. This source of strength proved to be a legislative weakness. The boards were abolished in 1870 on the heels of a sweeping Democratic party victory which restored a large measure of "home rule" to New York and Brooklyn.

This return to decentralization flew in the face of the increasing interdependence of the settlements in the metropolitan region. The costs of fragmentation rose steadily. Competitive development of the waterfront on both sides of the East River narrowed the channel and seriously restricted the current. Controls on the use of land in New York were difficult to enforce when nearby competitive areas were available for exploitation. The odors from manufacturing enterprises forbidden in the city were wafted across the harbor to mock the impotence of the New York Board of Health.[10]

The Census of 1880 described the cities of New York, Brooklyn, Jersey City, Newark, and Hoboken as "one great metropolitan com-

---

[9] "Annual Report of the Board of Commissioners of the Metropolitan Police," *New York Assembly Documents*, 93rd session, 1870 (Albany, 1870), Vol. II, no. 17, deals with the problems of the ferry connection.

[10] Charles A. Graham, Engineer in Chief, to Eugene Lynch, Secretary of the Dock Commission, March 16, 1875, Mayors Papers, Box 65; *New York Tribune*, June 16, 23, and 29, 1877; April 24, 1878.

munity."[11] The census takers were premature. The New York region was composed of competitive settlements vying for advantage. They lacked the institutional arrangements and the channels of communication which would have allowed them to act together to forward the well being of the entire area.

New York City, the principal competitor in the region, lacked these institutions and channels even within its own limited boundaries.

The geographic center of New York's population in 1870 was located roughly at Union Square at 14th Street. Eighty-five per cent of the city's inhabitants lived within two miles of the center; only 5 per cent lived farther than three miles. For most of the city's inhabitants, the scale of distances were even smaller. Nearly half of the population lived in the narrow belt, one and one-quarter miles long, between Canal and 14th Streets.

So near, and yet so far. The difficulties which plagued the movement of information also spread New York's districts far apart in space. The crucial difficulties lay in the streets. In the absence of radio and telephone communication, there were very few alternatives in New York to direct personal contact for the transmission of information between individuals. The limits of transportation were also the limits for communication.

No one in New York had a good word for its thoroughfares. They seemed in many places, as the Commissioner of Public Works put it, to be designed to "impede rather than to facilitate travel."[12] No one moved above the streets, no one below them. Vehicles of every description and function crowed together in the same narrow thoroughfares. There were no limited access highways, no special truck routes. No Manhattan rail connections served the docks. Cargo and passengers were forced into the same struggling line of movement. (A city ordinance of 1867 excluded swine from the built-up sections.) Wooden planks split under the pressure of a business traffic for which they were never intended. Cobblestones

[11] United States Bureau of the Census, *Tenth Census of the United States: 1880*, XVIII, "Report on the Social Statistics of Cities" (Washington, D. C., 1886), p. 531.
[12] Commissioner of Public Works George Van Nort to Mayor Havemeyer, April, 1874, Mayors Papers, Box 223.

were torn loose faster than they could be replaced. New Yorkers, threading their path through the pock-marked roadways, feared for their horses' legs. One slip and a valuable investment (with a longer life-expectancy than the modern automobile) was ruined beyond repair.

Life overflowed the houses and shops into the streets. Merchants spread their wares across the sidewalks. Pedestrians and shoppers stepped gingerly into the roadway. Parked horse-drawn and hand trucks imposed their own rest on other vehicles which were slowed to a crawl in the narrowed channels. Housewives, hard-pressed to get about, stayed close to home in the course of their daily shopping. To meet their needs, retailing was decentralized and retailers were mobilized. Peddlers, trying to expand the size of their potential market, roamed the city. Their carts in many places transformed channels of movement into stationary market places. The streets leading into the decrepit buildings of the old public markets were almost totally blocked. Market and street became one.[13]

Filth, snow, and ice accumulated in the streets to imperil health and inhibit movement. The thoroughfares, a legislative committee insisted in 1868, were clearly not "conveniently passable." The Mayor was constantly beseiged by complaints that one street or another was totally closed by accumulated filth. The paved roads were periodically cleaned by a private contractor but his fee was not sufficient to pay for even weekly cleaning throughout the city and for the removal of snow and ice. Mayor John Hoffman, testifying before the 1868 committee, doubted that even larger appropriations would yield substantial improvements. The contractor's interest in increasing his profits could not be reconciled with a complete dedication to cleanliness.[14]

Some of the difficulties which plagued movement along the streets stemmed from the barriers to the movement of sewage below the surface. New York's sewers prior to 1865 were a patch-

[13] "Report of the Board of Health of the Health Department of the City of New York for the Three Months Ending July 31st, 1873," Mayors Papers, Box 163.
[14] "Report of the Committee on Municipal Affairs Relative to Street Cleaning in New York City, April 30, 1868," *New York Senate Documents*, 91st Session, 1868 (Albany, 1868), Vol. I, no. 7, pp. 86, 17.

work of pipes laid independently and haphazardly at the initiative of local property owners. They were too narrow for the load imposed upon them and improperly embedded in the ground. Mains, laid to minimize costs, opened into the rivers at the points nearest their origins, rather than at a few central locations. Attempts were made after 1865 to reorganize the sewerage system but they were directed principally toward providing for the needs of the new areas. In the region below 14th Street, the sewers continued to clog and break, spewing their contents onto the roads and suffusing the roadbeds. Narrow pipes could not hold the water and after a heavy rainstorm even a major avenue like Broadway was turned into a "sluggish stream of deep brown mud." Construction in the older sections of the city was hampered by the lack of maps locating the pipes.[15] As with many more complex problems, the malady had to be appropriately described before it could be cured.

Horse-drawn streetcars, moving through the obstacle courses of the streets, were the major vehicles of mass transportation in the sixties. The cars of twelve separate companies wound their way through New York on twenty-one distinct routes at an average speed of four to six miles an hour. A handful of stage coach lines, legacies of an era which had passed, competed for traffic on Broadway, where real estate owners resisted the intrusion of the street railway tracks.[16]

The competitive companies clustered close to one another along the routes where the effective demand for their services promised the highest profits. This *economic* distribution of lines, undisturbed by legislative planning, left large sections of the city relatively isolated from one another. The great tenement district southeast of Union Square was laced with streetcar lines running south to the business center and north to the district's expanding edge where the tenements gave way to the shanties of land squat-

[15] Report on the Committee on Public Health, April 8, 1869, *New York Assembly Documents*, 92nd session, 1869 (Albany, 1869), Vol. X, no. 153, p. 3.

[16] Harry C. Carman, *The Street Surface Railway Franchises of New York City* (New York: Columbia University Press, 1919) describes the legislative history and routes of the street railways.

ters. (At the end of the tracks, the usual property rules were loosened.) Only with difficulty could the East Side tenement dwellers reach either the established districts or the growing edge of settlement on the other side of Broadway.

The statistical records of the sixties cannot tell us how many New Yorkers traveled on public transportation lines, how frequently they traveled, or how far. I have added the approximate number of passengers carried by the stage and street railway companies and divided this figure by the city's population. The quotient, 135 trips per person annually, totally ignores all travel by non-New Yorkers, including Brooklyn and New Jersey commuters. It also obscures the fact that many "trips" were counted more than once since they involved more than one transit line. The figure, crude and exaggerated, suggests that many New Yorkers, both adult and child, rarely ventured far from home. Their sphere of movement was circumscribed, their image of the city limited.[17]

Those who walked in the streets and rode the public transportation lines complained bitterly. The *Evening Post* indicted New York in 1867 as the "most inconveniently arranged commercial city in the world." A major portion of the indictment was directed at the streets and transit lines. The roads, the *Post* proclaimed, were "badly paved, dirty and necessarily overcrowded." The railway terminals were inconvenient and the street pavements were uneven. "The means of going from one part of the city to the other are so badly contrived that a considerable part of the working population . . . spend a sixth part of their working days on the street-cars or omnibuses, and the upper part of the city is made almost useless to persons engaged in any daily business of any kind. . . ."[18]

Movement was difficult and so New Yorkers clung together. In the tenement districts of the East Side, men were crowded at the rate of 250,000 to 300,000 to the square mile. Contiguity, however, did not solve the problems of communication between dis-

---

[17] I have used the official figures supplied by John I. Davenport, *Letter on the Subject of the Population of the City of New York, Its Density and the Evil Resulting Therefrom* (New York, 1867), p. 18.

[18] Quoted in Isaac Newton Phelps Stokes, *Iconography of Manhattan Island, 1498–1909* (New York: R. H. Dodd, 1918), III, pp. 757–758.

Squatters near Central Park, 1867: On the frontier of settlement the usual property rules were loosened. *Historical Pictures Service—Chicago*

tricts or even within neighborhoods extending beyond a block or two. The commissioners appointed in 1807 to design the upper city—roughly above Houston Street on the east and Gransevoort Street on the west—allowed for only a few public parks and squares. Land, they explained, was expensive, and they expected private homes and gardens to provide the social nexus of the new areas. After 1811, when their design was approved, the original allocation of open space was steadily reduced. Colonial merchants had leisurely searched for business information in the squares of the old city. The increasing frequency of business transactions and the growth of business reporting in the press destroyed their need and tolerance for scattered public centers.[19]

The creation of Central Park in 1857 reversed the trend to reduced public landholding. The Park did not, however, serve the functions of the older squares. It was designed not as an integral part but as a "relief" from urban existence.[20] It did not substantially affect the spatial or social organization of the crowded districts which housed most of the inhabitants of the city. With the notable exception of Tompkins Square on the East Side, the small squares in residential districts were ringed with fashionable homes. Men living only a few blocks apart in poorer areas, did not have a convenient public meeting place in which to gather and talk. Bars served as points of contact, but they were so numerous and so widely diffused that they confirmed, rather than broke, a pattern of intensely local social intercourse. The street plan itself had the same effect. The streets, laid out at right angles, had no focal points. They led to the river or to the horizon rather than to places of interest and communication. One block was the same as the next.

[19] Harold M. Lewis, *Physical Conditions and Public Services*, Regional Survey of New York and Its Environs, VIII (New York, 1929), pp. 156–162. The suggestion about the relation of urban design to the search for business information is an extension of the argument developed by Arthur H. Cole, "The Tempo of Mercantile Life in Colonial America," *Business History Review*, XXXIII (Autumn, 1959), pp. 277–299.

[20] "Letter to the Board of Commissioners of the Department of Parks from Frederick Law Olmsted and Calvert Vaux," Board of Commissioners of the Department of Public Parks, *Second Annual Report for the Year Ending May 1, 1872* (New York, 1872), p. 80.

These are the benchmarks and barriers of New York in 1870. It was a city extravagantly rich and desperately poor, democratic and unequal, exhilarating and enervating. Above all, New York was the center of a worldwide communications and transportation network that moved men, goods, and ideas and yet it suffered the costs of enormous barriers to movement within its own boundaries.

THREE

Communicating Across a Distance

The communications network of New York City severely limited face-to-face contacts between its inhabitants. The constraints on communication across a distance were equally restrictive. The revolution in postal service, to start with an obvious example of these constraints, was still in its infancy in 1870. Prior to 1863, the Post Office charged two cents for each letter delivered. The costs and uncertainty of delivery encouraged recipients of mail to purchase post office boxes where they could pick up their mail themselves. When Congress approved a system of free urban delivery in 1863, the number of post office boxes declined. The sorting of mail was simplified, the direct cost of service was reduced and the quality improved. Nevertheless, the Postmaster General complained in December, 1868, that New York still had 6000 boxes representing 30,000 names, "any one of which *each* sorting clerk must be able to recall and associate with the proper box on the instant, a work impossible to be done without liability to error." The post office was located in a dark and overcrowded seventeenth century church. The "liability to error" was increased by the surroundings.[1]

Postal service remained a source of bitter complaint. "You can send a letter to Boston, or Albany, or Chicago," one critic commented in 1869, "with a tolerable certainty of its reaching its destination. But if you mail a missive from your office in Pine or William Street to your friend in Gramercy Park, or Lexington Avenue . . . the chances of its ever being heard from are slight.

[1] United States Postmaster General, *Annual Report, 1868*, House Executive Documents, 40th Congress, 3rd Session, Vol. IV, no. 1, pp. 22, 31–32.

The time usually occupied *in transitu* between 'down' and 'uptown' is 24 hours to 24 days." [2]

The criticism may be exaggerated. The quality of "grumble" does not spoil the essential point. Only 6,000,000 local letters were delivered in the fiscal year 1867–1868. [3]

Communicating through the mails is at best slow and rather clumsy. If we could project ourselves back into the 1860's, the communications medium which we would miss the most, I suspect, would be the telephone. A great deal has been written about the impact of the automobile upon urban society, very little about the impact of the convenient, exciting, and annoying little black boxes. We can only guess at the measure of time and uncertainty which the absence of telephones added to the process of making decisions. The telegraph, which could, of course, convey information over a distance, could not cope with complex messages sent in great volume from person to person. Alexander Graham Bell's first advertisement for his new discovery in 1877 explained its virtues simply: "The communication is much more rapid, the average number of words transmitted in a minute by the Morse sounder being from fifteen to twenty, by telephone from one to two hundred." By 1880 the unruly and noisy New York central telephone exchange reported making 6,000 "communications" daily. [4]

The principal effect of the development of the telegraph was the creation of national and international markets in which local advantages were no longer secured by delays in the flow of information about the price and supply of commodities. The completion of the Atlantic cable and the extension of the continental telegraphic network in the sixties made Liverpool and New York prices known almost instantaneously in San Francisco, New Orleans and Minneapolis. New York was, for many purposes, more tightly linked to the outside world than it was internally united.

In one small way, the telegraph presaged the impact of the telephone upon the balance between competition and cooperation

[2] Junius Henri Browne, *The Great Metropolis, A Mirror of New York* (Hartford, Conn.: American, 1869), pp. 417–418.
[3] United States Postmaster General, *Annual Report, 1868*, p. 280.
[4] Herbert N. Casson, *The History of the Telephone* (Chicago: A. C. McClurg, 1910), p. 53: "The Telephonic Exchange in the United States," *Nature*, XXI (1880), p. 497.

within the city. In 1865 fire alarms in New York were still rung on bells from tall fire towers. The coded bell alarm, broadcast into the air for all to hear, identified the general district in which a blaze was located. Volunteer fire companies rushed to the scene in a mad competitive scramble for glory and monetary rewards. Fighting as they went, the companies frequently caused more damage than the flames they sought to douse.[5]

At the close of the Civil War, the New York Board of Fire Underwriters convinced the legislature that the city needed a professional fire corps. New public fire commissioners extended and improved telegraphic communication throughout the city and abolished the bell system. A network of fire boxes located the origin of an alarm precisely and indicated which companies were to fight the blaze. By 1873 there were 548 boxes on the island and 612 miles of wire.[6] Competitive units had been replaced by a new central agency with new capabilities. The professional fire department with the aid of the alarm boxes abandoned competition for profit as the incentive to effective fire fighting.

There were a great many different media in New York for communicating across a distance to a mass audience: daily and weekly newspapers, church and secular magazines, pamphlets, books and posted broadsides. In America, a British commentator noted in 1871, there is a "universality of print."[7] The flood of printed words could not, however, erase the barriers of ignorance that divided the city. The technical problems, structure, and character of the mass communications industry both influenced and measured the barriers of communication.

The problems of the daily newspapers were the most important in the industry. Rowell's American Newspaper Directory for 1870, one of the first attempts to list all American journals, described twenty-six dailies published in New York. There were eight major newspapers and eighteen smaller sheets, including several

---

[5] "Annual Report of the Metropolitan Fire Department, January 7, 1866," New York Assembly Documents, 89th Session, 1866 (Albany, 1866), no. 13, p. 12.
[6] Lowell M. Limpus, History of the New York Fire Department (New York: Dutton, 1940), pp. 263–264.
[7] Frank Luther Mott, American Journalism 3rd ed., (New York: Macmillan, 1962), p. 405.

of distinction. The *Sun, Herald,* and *Daily News* each commanded approximately ninety thousand readers. Between thirty and forty-five thousand purchased either the *Times, Tribune, World, Star,* or the German *Staats-Zeitung.*[8]

The newspapers were not very large. Copy was written and set by hand and papers were delivered in trucks with a low horse-power. The daily edition, therefore, could not readily exceed ten pages. Editors were attracted by news that could be gathered cheaply or for which they would be well paid. They exploited convenient news sources: legislative and court proceedings, official reports, public speeches and rallies. Lengthy extracts from governmental documents gave the papers a false air of realism. In fact, it was difficult to find out what was going on in Albany through the dull prose of the extracts from the Assembly or Senate journals.

The telegraph and the combined resources of the Associated Press made it easier for the papers to gather news from far away than from close to home. A contemporary critic, Junius Brown, captured this essential quality of the press. "Our night editors," he complained, "appear to think it of no consequence that a New Yorker has broken his neck, but of the greatest that a laborer on a Western railway or a freedman in Texas has been killed by a locomotive or a ruffian." [9]

The absolute number of newspapers in 1870 is particularly striking as New York in 1964 supports only five general English language dailies. The proliferation of journals a century ago tended to accentuate divisions within the city. Small, fiercely competitive journals have little market power (or, as newspaper men might prefer to call it, "editorial discretion") in the choice of the information they choose to sell. If they strike a false note, readers flee to the competitors. Larger papers in less competitive markets have more discretion and may simultaneously serve more diverse interests. Their monopolistic power makes them more effective agents of social integration.[10]

---

[8] George P. Rowell and Company, *American Newspaper Directory* (New York, 1870), pp. 698–699.

[9] Browne, *op. cit.,* pp. 417–418.

[10] There is no value judgment intended in this analysis. The social integration of a city left with only one newspaper is certainly won at a high cost if monopoly power is used to suppress ideas.

The operation of the newspapers as channels of communication was conditioned by bias in reporting. The enemies attacked on the editorial page were frequently ravaged even more decisively in the news columns. The infusion of editorial judgment into the news was probably less frequent in 1870 than it had been in 1850. The decline of bias was a measure of a profound social change; its persistence was a measure of the incompleteness of change.

Men in a society which respects tradition and hierarchy do not believe in "objective" facts.[11] The validity of a statement depends upon the authority of the speaker, not its independent "truth." The breakdown of the belief in authority is marked by an intense suspicion. Every statement appears as a pose for authority; every truth, a cloak for a personal or class interest. The belief that every statement is biased confirms itself. The reporter, certain that every other account is distorted, intertwines his moral judgments with the facts. The reader, convinced that the truth is uncertain, attaches himself to a comfortable moral and empirical statement.

This radical sociology of knowledge, which we associate with Karl Marx, appeared in almost every social group in the transformation of society in Europe and America. Suspicion shattered institutions and established ideas. Creatively, it generated a search for new facts, a new method for defining truth and new social organizations.[12]

In the world of the newspapers, the decline of suspicion was measured by the emergence of an ethic of objectivity and by the

[11] Ithiel de Sola Pool, "The Mass Media and Their Interpersonal Social Functions in the Process of Modernization," in Lewis Anthony Dexter and David Manning White, eds., *People, Society and Mass Communications* (New York: Free Press, 1964), pp. 433–437, makes a similar point but insists that "a criterion of objective truth . . . is one of the peculiar features of the Graeco-Roman Western tradition." My argument is that the development of this objective criterion was an integral part of the modernization of the West. It was not a legacy of the past (though the Greeks may have gone through a similar process of development) and was not equally respected throughout the population.

[12] Contrast the views on the freedom of intellectuals from class bias in Karl Marx and Frederick Engels, *The German Ideology, Parts I and II*, ed. R. G. Pascal (New York: International, 1947), pp. 27–43, and Karl Mannheim, *Ideology and Utopia*, trans. Louis Wirth and Edward A. Shils (New York: Harcourt, Brace, 1949), pp. 136–146.

rise in the social status of reporters. *The New York Times* in 1860 announced it intended "to publish *facts*, in such a form and temper as to lead men of all parties to rely upon its statements of facts, and then to discuss them in the light of truth and justice, and not of party interest." Whitelaw Reid, prior to assuming his responsibilities as editor of the *Tribune*, played on the same theme. "Independent journalism!" he wrote in 1872, "that is the watchword of the future in the profession! An end of concealments because it would hurt the party, an end of one-sided expositions . . . of doctoring the reports of public opinion . . . of half truths . . . that is the end which to every perplexed conscientious journalist a new and beneficent Declaration of Independence affords." [13]

The major barrier impeding the transition from suspicion to creative search, from bias to open communication, was persistent poverty and ignorance. New York shouted its poverty; the census takers recorded its ignorance. At least 43,000 persons above the age of ten could not read any language; 62,000 more could not write. (A still larger group was, of course, unable to read or write English.) American cities, the *Times* warned in 1871, were filled with men and women who "drudge year after year in fruitless labor. They never rise above their position; they see the gilded rewards of toil about them and can never grasp them. The employers and the rich seem to them heartless and selfish. In their blind and unconscious way, they feel themselves wronged and cheated by the comfortable classes of society. They long for a share in the luxuries which are always flaunted in their faces. They hate the rich. . . . They are densely ignorant and easily aroused by prejudice or passion." [14]

New Yorkers relied upon the schools to erase this ignorance and to integrate society. "Without the public schools," Mayor William Wickham said in 1876, "it might be doubted whether free institutions could long be maintained for a city like this." [15] The educa-

[13] *New York Times,* March 22, 1860; *Scribners Monthly, IV* (June, 1872), p. 204.
[14] *New York Times,* July 16, 1871.
[15] Mayor William Wickham, *Message to the Common Council, Board of Aldermen, January 3, 1876* (New York, 1876), p. 51.

tional institutions of the city could not, however, transcend the general social pattern. Their efforts, even with the young, were severely limited. Only 30 per cent of the students registered in the public schools appeared on an average day. Estimates of the number of children who never attended school ranged from the Board of Education's conservative ten or fifteen thousand upwards to sixty thousand. Most students ended their studies with the sixth grade. At that point, the Board of Education hoped, they could multiply and divide by two figures and had finished the second primer in one of the standard series.[16] The primers trained them to read out loud, trying to erase "verbal class distinctions," at the cost of speed. "Do not read too fast," Charles Saunders, the author of a popular series cautioned, "You should never read any faster than you could speak."[17]

The imagery and values of the school books were those of rural America. Even when the books turned cityward it was with a tone of studied condescension." There are thousands of poor people in the great cities," Willson's Second Reader of the School and Family Series (1860) explained. "We should be very thankful that our lot is better than theirs, but we should not be proud on account of our own better fortune. It was God alone who has made our lot to differ from the lot of theirs."[18]

The pedagogical tactics of the schools were not designed to alleviate the problem of irrelevant readings. The average class in the elementary grades was composed of fifty students. Teachers were asked to preserve strict discipline and to present an image of firm authority. Children, the school superintendent insisted in 1873, should "be early trained to habits of prompt obedience to

[16] Thomas Boese, *Public Education in the City of New York* (New York, 1869), pp. 126–13, 133–137. In 1876, 64 per cent of the students were in the first six grades, 79 per cent in the first eight. Board of Education, *Thirty-fifth Annual Report, For the Official Year Ending December 31, 1876* (New York, 1877), p. 120. The compulsory education act of 1874 had hardly made a dent on truancy in a city which had to turn away children for lack of space.

[17] Charles W. Saunders, *The School Reader, The Second Book* (New York, 1853), p. 19.

[18] Marcius Willson, *The Second Reader of the School and Family Series* (New York, 1860), p. 115.

teachers as well as to parents."[19] In this environment, teachers could not stop to explore their pupils' urban frames of reference or to promote analysis and self-expression. The curriculum remained out of touch with the student's needs—indeed, the needs of society at large.[20] Education, in the upper grades particularly, was still an obstacle course through which only the valiant and the hard-headed could pass. It was a barrier in front of the door of opportunity rather than a key.

There were profits to be reaped in New York for those who could improve communications. Newspapermen and inventors, struggling with writing machines and telephones, leaped to the bait. Educators, far from being in the vanguard of the communications revolution, more frequently presented major obstacles to its fulfillment. New Yorkers dreamed of communication through education; they invested in more immediately profitable media.

[19] Board of Public Instruction of the City and County of New York, *Thirty-first Annual Report, For the Year Ending December 31, 1872* (New York, 1873), p. 194.

[20] See the interview with former School Commissioner William Wood, *New York Tribune*, May 17, 1873. Some "practical courses" were introduced into the high school curriculum during the seventies. Board of Public Instruction, *Thirty-fifth Annual Report, 1876*, pp. 124–125.

FOUR

Communication and Organization

The last two chapters argued that the miserable streets, rigid schools, erratic mail delivery and biased newspapers of New York inhibited the development of a rich associational life, leaping over the boundaries of confined local attachments. The argument, phrased in this way, is obviously too simple. The pattern of associations was what might be called a mediating variable, reflecting but also altering the impact of the physical media, dependent upon their capacity to transmit information but also stimulating improvements in this capacity.

This mediating role is clear if we examine some of the institutions in which men struggled with the inadequacies of the communications network: charities, churches, and business firms.

Relief agencies sensed that they stood outside of the world of the poor. They needed more information about the men, women, and children they hoped to serve. Compare the problems of the well-established Association for Improving the Condition of the Poor (A.I.C.P.) with those of a business firm producing a conventional product. The A.I.C.P. wanted to know how much a man lacked; the firm, simply how much he was willing to spend. Market research was more difficult for philanthropists than for businessmen. The A.I.C.P. visitors, checking on each applicant for aid, were resented for prying. Fear of violence effectively closed many districts to inquiring almoners.[1]

For charity workers to increase the knowledge at their command, they had to alter the structure of their industry to allow

[1] Association for Improving the Condition of the Poor, *Twenty-sixth Annual Report, 1869* (New York, 1869), pp. 29–30.

27

for larger and more effective investments in information. The "relief industry" was composed of many small, uncoordinated, and even competitive "firms." Relief officials thought that the competitive structure of their industry increased the costs of their agencies unnecessarily, to the detriment of society at large and the poor. The "buyer" of relief could tell his sad story to several agencies and obtain aid several times over. The buyer, charity workers insisted, should be allowed to purchase welfare from only one seller. In the last three decades of the nineteenth century these good souls tried to unite, like businessmen in their fields, in order to exercise monopoly power. Their first efforts were directed at lowering the barriers to communication between agencies, developing common criteria for relief, collating files to eliminate duplication, and consolidating facilities to reduce costs.[2] In the second stage, the charitable agencies through settlement houses and social surveys, turned to an intensive study of their consumers' habits. Paradoxically, as they attempted to explore the land of the poor, they helped the poor to discover themselves. The settlement house united neighbors who had never spoken to each other; the surveys demonstrated the brotherhood of those who had appeared to suffer under purely local ills.[3]

The development of monopoly in the relief industry was plagued by difficulties which reflected the barriers to communication in society at large. The A.I.C.P., for example, suspiciously refused to share its files with other agencies.[4] At the same time, these very difficulties forced relief workers to improve communication. A united effort to deal with the poor required cooperation among the well-to-do. The *have's* could only extend an effective hand, or a word, to the *have-not's* after they had enriched the network of social communication among themselves.

[2] Marvin E. Gittleman describes the major limitations of the charity movement as a link between classes. "Charity and Social Classes in the United States," *American Journal of Economics and Sociology*, XXII, 2, 3 (April and July, 1963), pp. 313–329, 417–426.

[3] Lillian D. Wald, *The House on Henry Street* (New York: Henry Holt, 1915) is an ode to this effect. See her concluding sentences, p. 310. David Brody, *Steelworkers in America; The Nonunion Era* (Cambridge: Harvard University Press, 1960), pp. 159–164, describes the impact of the Pittsburgh Survey.

[4] *New York Tribune*, March 13, 1875.

The confrontation with poverty had the same effect in the churches that it had in the relief agencies. It impelled the upper and middle classes to coordinate their disparate activities. Here, too, the mediating role of associational life was apparent. The structure of the churches reflected the barriers to communication (some would say, "glorified" them).[5] At the same time, the churches were centers of the movement to expand the communications network.

Protestant churches, like the relief agencies, may usefully be compared to business firms. Over the course of several decades, these religious businesses had migrated northward. They moved as discrete and frequently competitive units to uptown locations where the effective monetary demand for their services was the greatest. As early as 1847 the editor of the *Princeton Review* noted sadly that the Presbyterian churches belonged to the men who paid the bills. The churches were private property, "intended for the cultivated and thriving classes of the city," and effectively excluding the great mass of the poor.[6]

Morgan Dix, rector of Trinity Church, surveyed his institution's lonely splendor in the lower city in 1871 and inveighed against the "stunted and cramped temper of congregationalism" which had abandoned "great and populous districts to Mammon and Care." The Episcopal Church to which Trinity belonged, had more hierarchical elements than any Protestant denomination in the city. Nevertheless, Dix pointed out, decisions were not centrally coordinated. "When the idea of Catholicity is lost," he warned, "when churches are regarded as the property of migratory individuals; when they are the private chapels and oratories of their wealthy pewholders; when the priests are but the chaplains of a few families whose names they keep in a little visiting book . . . and when the priest no longer realizes that he has any duties or relations to the ignorant, the ungodly, and the unhappy around his doors; then must such changes come as those which have occurred in New York." [7]

[5] This is the major indictment of denominationalism in H. Richard Niebuhr, *The Social Sources of Denominationalism* (New York: Henry Holt, 1929).
[6] Quoted in "Religion in New York," *Catholic World*, III (June, 1866), p. 383.
[7] Morgan Dix, *Address, Ascension Day, A.D. 1871, Trinity Church, New York* (New York, 1871), p. 6.

The "private chapels" which Dix condemned were centers of intense communication for small communities. In the vestry of his own church gathered one of the most prestigious "clubs" in the city which included, as part of an interlocking directorate, many trustees of Columbia College. John D. Rockefeller, though he was speaking about his Cleveland experiences, probably expressed a very general feeling of gratitude for the social life of the big city church. He liked best, he said, to mix with the "earnest and inspired people" of his congregation. He looked upon them, Allan Nevins tells us, as a "sodality," united by the "bonds of Christian affection." New York philanthropist James Stokes urged his son to "come out on the Lord's side," and join the society which was "more pleasant and profitable than that of the worldly." [8]

In the decade after the Civil War, Protestant churches in New York City joined in a national movement to coordinate their activities and to expand their mission to the poor. James E. Yeatman of St. Louis, an early leader in this movement of consolidation, acutely described the difficulties of the urban churches in his first *Circular of Inquiry*. The churches were frustrated by "want of knowledge of their moral condition; lack of organization of the wealth, piety and labor which exist there; need of experimental knowledge of the best agencies and how to perfect organizations already formed; and want of trained, tried, permanent laborers in the various spheres of city labor." [9]

In response to Yeatman's circular, a convention of prominent clergymen and laymen met in Cleveland in 1865. They established a permanent commission which gathered information on the activities of urban churches. Successive conferences attacked the foundations of Protestant decentralization. Membership in one congregation, Charles Hodge of Princeton insisted in New York in 1874, opened membership in every congregation. Non-sectarian

[8] Allen Nevins, *John D. Rockefeller* (New York: Scribner's 1940), II, pp. 119–120; Anna Bartlett Warner, *Some Memories of James Stokes and Caroline Phelps Stokes, Arranged for their Children and Grandchildren* (privately printed, n.p., 1892), p. 255.
[9] Aaron I. Abell, *The Urban Impact of American Protestantism, 1865–1900* (Cambridge; Harvard University Press, 1943), p. 11.

cooperation, ardent evangelists urged, was the way to a rebirth of apostolic Christianity which would reach the isolated poor.[10]

To meet the challenge of the poor, the separate denominations in the seventies, led by Dix's Episcopal Church, organized unifying alliances and conferences on both a city-wide and national basis. The Episcopalians, historian Aaron Abell writes, "found in missionary topics a bond of common interest before which theological differences receded into the background." [11]

The Protestant churches of New York in 1870 were involved in the beginnings of a communications revolution which, in the decades to come, would increase their own internal unity, their knowledge of the poor and the lines which linked social classes. The young revolution in 1870 had hardly begun to solve the problems which Yeatman described: lack of knowledge, organization, and personnel.

One special personnel problem loomed in Yeatman's mind as particularly important and it deserves special mention. In our society, the tasks which are not rewarded in the market are performed by the rich, the dedicated, and the free. Women, as a group, are more likely to enjoy one or more of these qualities than are men. The church, Yeatman argued, needed more female workers to carry a message for which, unfortunately, there was no effective monetary demand.

New York in 1870 did not, however, have a large corps of independent women. Women were more isolated than any other group in the city with the possible exception of the class of vagrant men, women, and children who were without homes and almost totally without roots. The suffrage movement hardly penetrated the dense walls which circumscribed female life. Women were tightly locked in the narrow circle of home and family. Eighty-six thousand were in the labor force but three quarters of these female workers were engaged in the small world of domestic servants, laundresses, seamstresses and dressmakers. Women were virtually unknown in the banking and insurance houses of the city. Only 5 per cent of the "clerks, salesmen and accountants" in the stores of New York wore skirts.

[10] *Ibid.,* pp. 12–17.
[11] *Ibid.,* p. 17.

The barriers which isolated women from each other and from the larger male society were clearly beginning to crack in 1870. Sorosis, the first general women's club in the city, was two years old and though it was still small it heralded a new world to come.[12] The State Charities Aid Association, with strong feminine leadership, was organized in 1870 and played an important role in shaping social welfare policy in subsequent decades.[13] The Protestant call to recruit female workers—and the parallel call in business firms—opened new opportunities for women and encouraged them to leave the confined quarters of their homes.

The women's response to these new calls was slowed by their inefficiency at home. The continuing isolation of women—and hence the inability of society to use them outside the home—stemmed, at least in part from their ignorance of "domestic science." They did not know how to improve their productivity. In the sixties and seventies, a growing flood of articles and manuals offered the housewife the benefits of a new wisdom. The most famous of these manuals, *The American Woman's Home*, by the Beecher sisters, suggested methods of increasing productivity similar to those which Frederick Winslow Taylor later urged upon businessmen in the name of scientific management. The Beechers proposed to economize "time, labor and expense," by "close packing of conveniences," and new systems to budget time and money and to organize the work process.[14]

Women used their new freedom and new time in many ways. They raised the standard of cleanliness, learned new recipes, read romantic novels and fretted with their appearance. A great many women joined a network of social clubs which were designed, in part, to "use time," in part, to "do good." A small but significant group dedicated their efforts to re-allocating the distribution of social welfare dictated by the market place. Women, comparatively free of the need to earn their living in the market, vigorously supported the countless reform activities

[12] Mrs. J. C. Croly, *The History of the Woman's Club Movement in America* (New York, 1898), pp. 15–27.
[13] David M. Schneider and Albert Deutsch, *The History of Public Welfare in New York State* (Chicago; University of Chicago Press, 1941), pp. 20–22.
[14] Catherine E. Beecher and Harriet Beecher Stowe, *The American Woman's Home* (New York: J. B. Ford, 1869), pp. 13, 25, 222.

of the Progressive period.[15] In 1870 women were not available in great numbers to staff agencies whose efforts the market would not reward and to publicize messages for which no one would pay. Without active women working in the community, New York in 1870 necessarily depended more than it did in 1900 upon decisions made in the market place.

The Catholic Church, to return to the religious organizations with which we began, prided itself that it had not lost contact with the "idea of Catholicity." Protestants occasionally looked upon their abandoned mother church with envy. "Realized, working Christianity," James Parton wrote in the *Atlantic Monthly* in 1868, may be uniquely viewed in one of New York's "densely peopled Catholic parishes, where all is dreary, dismal desolation excepting alone in the sacred enclosure around the church, where a bright interior cheers the leisure hours; where pictures, music, and stately ceremonial exalt the poor above their lot; and where a friend and a father can ever be found." [16]

The Catholic Church, despite its pride, was clearly aware of its own limitations. One third of the Catholic population, a friendly author estimated in 1866, never attended mass. He attributed their absence principally to "poverty, discouragement, indolence and a careless habit or some other reason which does not imply loss of faith." John McCloskey, the new Archbishop of New York, reduced the size of the city's parishes in 1864 and increased the number of churches. He hoped to relieve overcrowding and to allow the clergy to "learn to know not only those who came spontaneously to the offices of the Church and the duties of religion, but also the careless and indifferent." [17]

Despite its pride, the Catholic Church was not a perfectly free and open medium of communication. It, too, reflected and, at the same time, struggled against, the barriers in the greater

[15] George E. Mowry, *The Era of Theodore Roosevelt and the Birth of America, 1900–1912*, New American Nation Series (New York: Harpers, 1958), pp. 33–37.

[16] James Parton, "Our Roman Catholic Brethren," *Atlantic Monthly*, XXI (May, 1868), p. 565.

[17] "Religion in New York," *Catholic World*, III (June, 1866), p. 387; John G. Shea, *The Catholic Churches of New York* (New York, 1878) is testimony to McCloskey's enterprise.

society. The Catholic school system, with only 20,000 students, was still very small. The lines of connection between districts were clerical and narrow. The priests of the sixties, a sympathetic Catholic author argued, commanded little respect in the general community and showed little concern with the "great moral demonstrations of the day." They focused their attention upon the "immediate and temporal wants of their own people." [18]

The major interparish Catholic lay organization was the Society of St. Vincent de Paul, which visited and relieved the poor and made a special effort to save vagrant children from the clutches of poverty, despair, and Protestants. The work of the society was restricted. Its members did not share the intense curiosity about poverty and sympathy for the poor which frequently characterized Protestant social missions. There were 932 members in the city in 1870, drawn largely from men who had succeeded after a life of struggle in obtaining "comparative ease." They could not be expected, the vice-secretary explained, to dwell upon the sufferings of the poor. They accepted poverty as a fact and believed any man could obtain ease if he worked hard.[19]

The Catholic clergy and the Society of St. Vincent de Paul were limited channels for the passage of information between classes. Capital did not flow any more freely than information. The Catholic Church, despite its hierarchy and its universality, shared many characteristics with Protestant denominations and charities. Each parish financed its own church, school, and welfare services with very little outside assistance or direction.[20] Channels of communication were narrow, knowledge was not widely diffused and decisions were made in a decentralized fashion close to the sources of information.

A primitive communications network affected the world of man's work, as well as God's. Printing and baking, clothing, machinery and cigar making, construction, and brewing were

[18] "Religion in New York" *Catholic World*, III (June, 1866), p. 387.
[19] *Reports of the Superior Council of New York to the Council General of the Society of St. Vincent de Paul at Paris for the Year 1870* (New York, 1871), p. 18.
[20] James Parton, "Our Roman Catholic Brethren, I," *Atlantic Monthly*, XXI (April, 1868), pp. 444–445.

the staples of New York manufacturing.[21] In each of these industries, the characteristic firms were small so that owners and managers could directly coordinate their activities, Merchants and bankers with extensive business interests similarly got on with a handful of employees and relatively simple record keeping.

The leaders of the few large firms in the city with more than one hundred employees complained that their subordinates tended to violate central directives and to form firms within the firm. Railroad presidents, for example, frequently spoke of their inability to know what was going on down the line. Insurance executives, though proud and assertive in their business posture, could not control the far-flung activities of their own agents.[22] A major constraint limiting the size of most firms was the rapid rise in managerial costs as the enterprise grew larger and the need for complex information more intense.

In the last three decades of the nineteenth century, more and more businessmen came to share the problems of the large firms of 1870. Accordingly, entrepreneurs increased their investments in internal communications and techniques of coordination. Since planning in advance of need was beyond the capabilities of most businessmen, firms—like cities—were beset by severe administrative "uncoupling" before their several parts could be made to work together.[23]

In 1870 most industries were fiercely competitive. The competitive entrepreneurs did not freely share information or decide on common policy. Industrial trade associations were still in their infancy. Manufacturers' associations which were established to meet the challenge of organized labor were more unstable than

[21] Louis Hacker, Abraham Venitzky, and Dora Sandorawitz, "The Beginnings of Industrial Enterprise After the Civil War," Alexander C. Flick, ed., *History of the State of New York* (New York: Columbia University Press, 1937), X, pp. 3–35.

[22] Thomas Cochrane, *Railroad Leaders, 1845–1890, The Business Mind in Action* (Cambridge: Harvard University Press, 1953), pp. 54–51; Shepard Clough, *A Century of American Life Insurance, A History of the Mutual Life Insurance Company of New York, 1843–1943* (New York: Columbia University Press, 1946), pp. 163–165, 196–200.

[23] Joseph A. Litterer, "Systematic Management: Design for Organizational Recoupling in American Manufacturing Firms," *Business History Review*, XXXVII, 4 (Winter, 1963), pp. 369–391.

the unions they faced. The Chamber of Commerce represented only a small fraction of the entire merchant community. Large segments of the community—local produce distributors, for example—were untouched by attempts at organization. Even in industries formally regulated by the state, firms grew like Topsy, "out of knowledge," and out of control. The twenty new savings banks opened in the city between 1867 and 1870, each with a unique charter, totally overwhelmed the state commissioner. The banks were free to choose their investments and business procedures without bothering with Albany.[24]

The professions of medicine and law presented extreme cases of the breakdown of central control and the sharing of techniques and information. A long process of democratization had lowered the barriers to entry into the learned professions and destroyed the community of shared knowledge and tradition. In the Empire State, a physician complained in 1871, "the most ignorant boor has practically the same right to hang out the badge of our profession, as the man who has spent his patrimony, and the best years of his life, in acquiring a certain degree of mastery over its intricate problems." The new Bar Association formed in New York City in 1870 was faced with a similar decay of knowledge and control. It hoped that it could "give new life to traditions which we believe to be only dormant, not extinct." [25]

Scientific and trade journals were a very important but still very limited media for sharing information in 1870. During the seventies and eighties the United States witnessed a vast expansion of these technical and professional periodicals. The old standbys were deluged in a flood of new publications. For the first time, the production of newspapers and magazines began to out-run the rapid growth of population.[26] Before the flood, busi-

[24] Superintendent of the Banking Department, *Annual Report Relative to Savings Banks, Transmitted to the Legislature, March 13th, 1872* (Albany, 1872), pp. 9–10.
[25] *New York Medical Journal*, XIII (May, 1870), pp. 498–499; *Albany Law Journal*, I (March 12, 1870), pp. 203–204.
[26] Frank Luther Mott, *A History of American Magazines, 1885–1905* (Cambridge: Harvard University Press, 1957), pp. 11–12; Charles H. Judd, "Relation of School Expansion to Reading," *Elementary School Journal*, XXIII (December, 1922), pp. 253–255.

nessmen were forced to act independently, reproducing innovations which had already been achieved and deciding their future behavior under conditions of extreme uncertainty.[27]

Some businessmen in New York clung to the benefits of a limited communications and transportation network. Difficulties of movement gave many retail distributors, for example, sufficient locational advantages to wield monopolistic power in the market place. They resisted improvements in transportation and as the century went on they attacked the growth of the central market district and the department stores as instruments of despotism.

A strange twist on this insistence on limited communication served to unite the merchant community. Merchant shippers organized in the seventies to prevent the major railroads from cooperating with each other. At the beginning of the decade there were five major roads from the eastern seaboard to the Midwest. "Five great railroads to New York," William Vanderbilt said in 1877, "with only business enough for two.[28] The roads fluctuated between intense rate wars and formal and informal cooperative price-setting in a manner characteristic of oligopolies. The usual pattern of railroad pooling arrangements (the best example was the compact reached in 1877) involved the equalization of rates from Liverpool, or London, to Chicago on all of the lines. The special claims of New York to cheaper rates, on the grounds that the size of its market yielded economies of scale, were denied.

Merchant shippers joined in protest. New York's competitive position would be improved, they argued, if railroad executives were forbidden to share price information. The city's locational advantages would be preserved.[29]

[27] W. Paul Strassman, *Risk and Technological Innovation: American Manufacturing Methods During the Nineteenth Century* (Ithaca; Cornell University Press, 1959), pp. 209–211. Strassman's image of the nineteenth century is very similar to that presented in these pages. "The picture of nineteenth-century American reflected by these industries," he writes, "is that of an economy remarkably flexible and unfettered by tradition, but, by the same token, poorly coordinated and without much liaison among groups with common interests," pp. 225–226.

[28] *New York Times*, March 31, 1877.

[29] This is the basic theme of Lee Benson, *Merchants, Farmers and Railroads* (Cambridge, Harvard University Press, 1955).

In most circumstances, New York businessmen favored—even if they were incapable of accomplishing—an improvement of communication. The dominant movement in American business organization in the late nineteenth century was to improve communication by merging firms, transforming competitive into coordinated units. In 1870, the improvement of communication was designed not so much to reduce competition as to improve it.

Businessmen in New York usually informed themselves about the state of the market by sticking close to their competitors. Proximity offered advantages which even a newspaper list of current-prices could not offer. Dry goods dealers and leather merchants clustered together in their ghetto-like districts. A deviant leather manufacturer moving from the Swamp, as their area was known, risked total loss of contact with his customers and the customers of other firms. The advantages of staying close to the market far exceeded the costs of additional competition.[30]

By the middle of the nineteenth century, the city had grown too big for immediate personal contact to serve the needs of many industries. The northward expansion of the waterfront on both sides of Manhattan and the diffusion of mercantile activity throughout the metropolitan region destroyed the tight little merchant community of the early nineteenth century. Produce merchants involved principally in international trade responded by replacing the informal exchange of information with a formal central market in the 1850's. This new Corn Exchange was quickly overcrowded. After the war, the merchants reorganized themselves and constructed enlarged quarters. The Produce Exchange opened in 1873 with 2,237 members. Cotton merchants and "importers and grocers" organized similar central markets during the seventies. Cooperation to perfect the market place brought merchants together to share the costs of expanded reporting services. Their own business interests led them to improve the network of social communication.[31]

[30] This clustering of communication-oriented industries is discussed in Edgar M. Hoover and Raymond Vernon, *Anatomy of a Metropolis* (Cambridge: Harvard University Press, 1959), pp. 62–73.

[31] Richard Edwards, *New York's Great Industries* (New York, 1884), pp. 65–78; Produce Exchange, *Annual Report for 1873–'74* (New York, 1874), pp. 17–22.

Perfection of price information in the import and export markets came quickly. Changes in the securities market, which required fundamental alterations in American business practice, evolved more slowly. Rumor, or "inside-dope," on the one side and ignorance on the other are, even today, the basis for a substantial proportion of stock market operations. In 1870, in the absence of standard corporate reporting, investment decisions rested almost entirely on inadequate information. Stock brokers asked repeatedly, but unsuccessfully, for state action to require fuller reporting.[32]

The pattern of city life thus included a major dynamic element. New Yorkers interacted actively with one another and yet decisions were decentralized. The gap between the level of actual connection and the level at which decisions were made was a product of a primitive communications network. The gap induced a series of increasing costs, felt both by the citizenry as a whole and by special groups and organizations. If information had been free, these costs might have been promptly met. Since the development of a communications network and of techniques of dealing with complex data was, in fact, very costly, there was an inevitable lag. However roughly estimated, the price at which knowledge could be bought had to be less than the costs of ignorance before a change could be effected.

[32] The *Commercial and Financial Chronicle* was a consistent spokesman for the advocates of mandatory reporting. See, for example, VII (December 26, 1868), pp. 813–814; X (January 15, 1870), p. 70.

FIVE

The Democratic Dream

Government, politics, and the dream of a democratic society cut through the maze of communication lines to touch almost everyone in New York. The policeman, the wardheeler, and the street-corner agitator spread their web over the population. Their activities helped to unite a fragmented city, to suppress the social conflict and the dissolution which the jeremiahs prophesied would be the civic fate.

A wide variety of critics attested to the role of democratic politics in reinforcing social harmony and preserving law and order. Paradoxically, their testimony was frequently part of a diatribe against politicians. Reformers charged that the city was ruled by scoundrels who catered to the ignorant and lawless masses.[1] Radicals of the Left berated the working class for its blind allegiance to parties dominated by capitalists.[2] Both arguments revealed the poor engaged by a political system which encouraged neither violence nor revolution.

Political institutions promoted order and stability on three levels. On the most obvious and formal plane, conflicts were resolved by the give and take through which government agencies reached decisions. The lower class shared only marginally in this process. The limitations on its participation were obscured by the elaborate ceremonies of conventions, campaigns, and elections. Democratic political rituals were more important as affirmations of faith in the Republic than as precise contributions to the process of governing.

[1] See the circular issued by the New York Municipal Society, *New York Tribune*, November 1, 1877.
[2] *Labor Standard*, October 28, 1877.

40

On a second level, the coal at Christmas time, the picnics, and the accent of the local political leaders suggested a benevolence which was not part of the formal governmental system. They also had the natural effect of making the participants in local politics feel that the area in which personal associations were fullest was the most important area of political decision-making. The ward bosses, the place seekers, and the hangers-on at the local political clubs, a hostile critic observed, were infatuated with the possibilities of politics. Local leaders tended to conceive of every governmental act as somehow related to partisan advantage and their own activities and welfare.[3] Insofar as they communicated that delusion, they contributed to the stability of society.

Politicians worked actively and sometimes illicitly to give their constituents a sense of political importance. The number of eligible voters in the city jumped from 17.75 per cent of the population in 1865 to 22 per cent in 1875, close to the proportion expected in a native-born population. The increase was caused in part by the massive and largely fraudulent naturalization proceedings undertaken by the Democratic Party between 1868 and 1870.[4] Men who have a sense of participation in government are less likely to riot than men who have a feeling of political impotence. Certainly, the extension of the franchise contributed to the sense of participation.

Politicians "educated" the public in political amenities. Even when they spoke of a war of classes their analysis had an essentially distracting quality. They placed all the "oppressors of labor" in the other party, suggesting that major social changes could be accomplished by a proper vote.[5] They insisted that the workingman had a stake in the standard political issues such as the currency, tariff, reconstruction, and corruption and repelled suggestions that these issues were only the concern of businessmen.[6]

At yet a third level, democratic politics encouraged stability

[3] Henry D. Bellows, Civil Service Reform (New York, 1877), pp. 7–9.
[4] Henry Davenport, The Election Frauds of New York City and Their Prevention (New York, 1881).
[5] See the Democratic speeches reported in the New York Tribune, October 3, 1873.
[6] Congressman Fernando Wood rejected proposals for a special labor commission on these grounds. Congressional Globe, 42 Cong., 2nd. session, 100:223.

because it promised eventual peaceful victory to the most out-spoken critics of the social and economic systems. The nineteenth century was the age of the citizen. The relationship of one man to another as members of the political community was charged with an intense moral meaning and value, while other relationships suffered in prestige. The rules which defined the behavior to one another of rich and poor, master and servant, members of the same craft and even parents and children were regarded, in comparison with the emergent values attached to citizenship, as transitory and without a stable moral worth.[7]

The idea of citizenship compensated, to some degree, for the earlier weakening of other communal ties. Citizenship and the rules attributed to the political community were also weapons in the attack against these ties. The attack was launched on the lofti-est level in the ringing phrases of the French "Declaration of the Rights of Man and of the Citizen." On a humbler, but perhaps more important level, enormous social changes were justified by demands that the new political community be preserved. The strikes of 1872, the *Commercial and Financial Chronicle* charged, were led by "turbulent men" and "noisy demagogues of foreign birth" who had "scarcely become identified with the institutions of a country where the workman is a citizen enjoying equal politi-cal rights with the most wealthy capitalist."[8] Considerations of "sentiment" must never invade governmental policy, the *Tribune* argued in February, 1877.[9] Republican Assemblyman Thomas Alvord similarly announced "It is not the duty of government to take care of the laborers. Least of all should a government do so after being threatened with disruption if it did not. Such compli-ance would quickly change the form of government. The doctrine that a government must provide work for unemployed laborers was not republican."[10]

The basic stability of New York society was ensured by the fact that the most radical critics of the course of economic and so-

---

[7] Reinhard Bendix, "The Lower Classes and the 'Democratic Revolution'," *Industrial Relations*, I (October, 1961), pp. 91–116, presents a similar argument.

[8] *Commercial and Financial Chronicle*, XV (July 13, 1872), p. 389.

[9] *New York Tribune*, February 24, 1877.

[10] *New York Tribune*, February 19, 1877.

cial change accepted the promises of participation in the democratic process, and city workingmen remained faithful to the existing parties.

The radical critics understood the character of the process to which they were committed. Gustav Schwab, the most picturesque New York communist (his tavern was one of the "sights" of the city), was essentially correct in 1877 when he described the capitalists as "revolutionaries," using the instruments of government to aid their sweeping transformation of social relations.[11] When their prerogatives were threatened by violence, the whole weight of the state was used to assert that no issue took precedence over the maintenance of order and the rule of law. Governor Robinson warned strikers on the Erie Railroad in 1877, to abandon their attempts to stop the trains. They had no proprietary rights in their jobs and no authority to interfere with non-striking workers. "It is no longer a question of wages," he said, "but of the supremacy of the law, which protects alike the lives, the liberty, the property and the rights of all citizens. To the maintenence of that supremacy, the whole power of the state will be invoked if necessary."[12]

This radical faith in the potential worth of political action lessened both the danger of violence in the city and the actual possibility of dramatically changing the economic or social order. Three times in the seventies discontented workingmen threatened violent riots against the institutions of the city. Three times, the leaders of the discontented men refused the barricade in favor of the long, peaceful, and compromising road represented by the ballot box and the rule of law.

The first incident was in the spring of 1872. Sixty thousand men left their jobs in May and June to press for a uniform eight-hour day and enforcement of the state eight-hour laws. Strikers and police clashed repeatedly. Crowds gathered around the Steinway piano factory to urge the workers to walk out and they were met by club-wielding policemen. The response of the strikers' leaders was unvarying. At a meeting in City Hall Park in the first stages of the strike, one speaker told the audience that the workers

---

[11] *New York Tribune*, July 26, 1877.
[12] *New York Tribune*, September 23, 1877.

were politically capable of carrying any measure they pleased. "You are seven-eighths of the voters of this country, and if you only will it you can shape the Government and shape the Legislature, irrespective of the Republican or the Democratic Party." He confidently warned the police that the workingmen were the "power that created them, and the power that created them can remove them." The strikers appealed to the Governor and he politely ordered an investigation. The strike had collapsed before the investigators could marshall their facts. The eight-hour statutes remained unenforced.[13]

A year and a half later, on January 13, 1874, ten thousand marchers trooped to Tompkins Square to demand that the authorities provide them with jobs. The police attacked the crowd. The attack was answered by an assertion of the rights of free assembly and speech and not by retaliatory violence. John Swinton, a radical journalist, delivered the principal address at a protest meeting on January 30. He spoke of the Tompkins Square "outrage." "I saw the wretched masses who then gathered there, and it seemed to me that only men utterly demoralized could have acted toward them as our authorities did." He went on to denounce the evils of the economic and political system. "The power of money has become supreme over everything. It has secured for the class which controls it all the special privileges and special legislation which it needs to secure its complete and absolute domination."

After a bitter tirade, Swinton cautioned against rebellion. "There must be no violence in the assertion of popular rights," he warned. "Law is the first argument and last appeal in this country, but the freedom of meeting and of speech must be maintained." Politicians, he concluded, must be queried about their willingness to uphold free speech.

The final opportunity to go to the barricades came in 1877, probably the first year in the history of the nation in which the supremacy of law and the ability of employers to use the government to protect the free market place and enforce industrial discipline was seriously tested by violence and threats of violence on a national scale. Riots erupted in Baltimore, Pittsburgh, San Francisco, Chicago, St. Louis, and Toledo. Strikers barred the

[13] *New York Tribune*, May 28, June 6, and July 6, 1872.

tracks of the great eastern railroads. New York officials trembled. The National Guard was called to duty and the police were alerted. The Mayor, though severely criticized for lack of prudence, did not attempt to halt the rallies of the unemployed. They were not forced into extra-legal action.[14]

There was no violence in New York. David Conroy, a labor union leader, opened a giant rally on July 25 at the heat of the crisis. "I hope and trust that you, fellow citizens and workingmen," he began, "will show to the press of New York tonight that you are an orderly people and that you are no rioters." Even the more radical speakers concluded by urging the formation of a workers political party. Nothing will be gained by strikes now, Gustav Schwab told a newspaper reporter. Time and hard work will be necessary to organize the workers and to elect the proper men to the legislature.

The radicals believed that political society in New York was open to change and therefore amenable to manipulation. Their premise was right; their conclusion ironically mistaken. New York was open but the diffusion of power, the fragmentation of authority, and the breadth of opportunity made it difficult to reform or reconstruct the city.

[14] Robert V. Bruce, *1877: Year of Violence* (Indianapolis: Bobbs-Merrill, 1959) describes the strikes.

SIX

Decentralized Government and

the Big Pay-Off

New York's preference for either weak or decentralized government was written on almost every aspect of the city's face. The preference was expressed in crime, in high public policy, and in the very structure of the municipal government.

Individuals were not overly restrained by legal rules in New York in 1870. Crimes against both person and property were probably more frequent than they were to be in the twentieth century.[1] The "nether side" of New York described by journalist Edward Crapsey in 1872 was a world apart, with its own rules of behavior and its own special ways of accommodating itself without conforming to the legal code.[2] New Yorkers tried, but they could not entirely contain the violence of the poor within their closed districts. The mayor's mail was filled with complaints about banditry in the streets.[3] George Templeton Strong, lawyer and diarist, was alarmed by the spread of "burglaries, highway robberies and murders." "Tonight's *Post*," he noted on February 12, 1869, "speaks of 'secret meetings of respectable citizens' and of Vigilance Committees already organized and ready for action in *this* ward and in another." New York's vigilantes never donned black masks to

[1] Daniel Bell, "The Myth of Crime Waves: The Actual Decline of Crime in the United States," *The End of Ideology* (Glencoe: Free Press, 1960), pp. 137–158.
[2] Edward Crapsey, *The Nether Side of New York* (New York: Sheldon, 1872).
[3] See the scattered letters on swindling and pocket-picking—the characteristic forms of urban banditry—in Box 213, Mayors Papers.

ride through the city streets on galloping horses. They did organize in frequent *ad hoc* citizen's committees and special associations empowered by the legislature to enforce the law.[4] It was difficult to know what rules to follow even if one was prepared to observe the law. Elliot Shepard, chairman of the Bar Association committee on codification, described the structure of laws and ordinances as a "most cumbersome, inconsistent and unreliable mass, from which lawyers and laymen alike can neither pick out the law or ordinance on any particular subject, nor recover from the fruitless effort without a sense of disgrace that so fair and great a city should be in such legal confusion and ruin."[5]

Disrespect for law merged into a general scorn for politics, government, and politicians. Businessmen tended to blame the government and politicians for introducing unnecessary, indeed the principal, uncertainties into enterprise. Politicians were derided as stupid demagogues, whose choice of a profession was almost certain evidence of venality. This derision, as historian Edward Chase Kirkland notes, was part of a "daydream" that government action did not involve genuinely divisive issues. Political uncertainties were charged to the politicians who "agitated" the public rather than to conflicts in the electorate.[6] Jacob Vermilye, president of the Merchants National Bank in New York, told the Senate Committee on Banking and Finance in 1878 that prosperity would return if only Congress would adjourn for three years. The policy of the Chamber of Commerce, one member suggested in 1875, "should be to urge the substitution of political economy for politics."[7]

[4] Allan Nevins and Milton Halsey Thomas, eds., *The Diary of George Templeton Strong* (New York: Macmillan, 1952), IV, p. 241. See Matthew J. Breen, *Thirty Years of New York Politics Up-to-Date* (New York, 1899), pp. 253–257 for a description of the threat of vigilantes and chapters 9 and 15 of this book for a discussion of citizens' groups.
[5] Eliot F. Shepard to Mayor William Wickham, February 25, 1875, Mayors Papers, Box 224.
[6] Edward Chase Kirkland, *Dream and Thought in the Business Community, 1860–1900* (Ithaca; Cornell, 1956), pp. 115–118.
[7] *New York Tribune*, May 3, 1878; *Eighteenth Annual Report of the Chamber of Commerce of the State of New York For the Year 1875–'76* (New York, 1876), p. 33.

Politicians were sensitive to the deprecation of their profession. Fernando Wood, congressman and former mayor, expounded in 1874 upon the "most dangerous existing obstacle in this country to the success of our experiment with free government." The obstacle was the "want of respect for authority—the lack of reverence, so to speak, for the public acts of those who make and those who enforce the laws." Condemn the legislator, Wood warned, and the law is degraded. The "wholesome restraints which the security of life and property require" are loosened. "Thus classes which, while under proper check, are harmless, become dangerous even to the foundation upon which rests the security of social order." Even the "more intelligent," Wood sadly noted, tended to encourage the general want of confidence in the "chosen rulers." The example of their scorn "operates prejudicially to their own interests in its demoralizing effect upon others who are less qualified to judge." [8]

The commitment both to decentralization and to a minimum of government intervention appeared on the highest levels of New York's choices in national affairs and conditioned the city's relations with the rest of the nation. The purpose of decentralization was in large part to reduce the city's need for information. Life was easiest when it took care of itself.

The impact of the demand for decentralization upon a complex interdependent system was most apparent in New York City's relations with the South, the poorest section of the nation. The Democratic Party in the city upheld "states rights" and local initiative and attacked federal attempts to reconstruct the former Confederate states. "Reconstruction," Congressman Samuel Cox told a New York audience, was the policy of the "Constitution-breaking, law-defying, negro-loving, Phariseeism of New England." [9]

New York Republicans were not far behind their Democratic colleagues. They consistently supported a "moderate" reconstruction policy and by 1875 had almost completely turned to oppose

[8] *Congressional Record*, 43rd Congress, 1st session, II, Part 1, p. 532.
[9] *Speeches of Hon. S. S. Cox in Maine, Pennsylvania and New York During the Campaign of 1868* (New York, 1868), p. 7.

federal coercion. William Dodge, President of the Chamber of Commerce, struck the characteristic note of Republican complaint. Capital would not enter the South, he insisted, unless businessmen were confident of political stability. Only state government based upon the consent of the people of the South, and not federal bayonets, could encourage confidence. The South, he concluded, must be left to work out its own problems.[10]

Opposition to Reconstruction was complemented by the consistent unwillingness of New York's representatives to support federal aid for Southern development. New York representatives, almost to a man, voted against subsidies for the Texas and Pacific Railroad, the construction of levees on the Mississippi, and the improvement of navigation on the lower portion of the river and its tributaries. "There is not a single measure of relief for the South and Southwest," a Southerner noted bitterly in 1876, "that has not been opposed by Tammany Hall." [11]

The policy of New York bankers expressed the same reluctance actively to encourage Southern development. This reluctance took the form of a demand for a simple uniform national banking system, rather than a demand for decentralization. Both responses—uniformity and decentralization—failed to grapple with the problems of the nation's poorest area.

At the close of the Civil War, the "underdeveloped" regions of the nation demanded that the banking system relieve their backwardness and encourage growth. In fact, the system adopted by Congress accentuated regional differences. The initial bank formula of 1865 distributed the greatest proportion of the allowable bank circulation to the richer states. The formula ignored the fact that the business of the highly developed regions was relatively independent of bank notes. Businessmen in the Northeast relied largely upon checks and other credit devices. The poorer sections with limited banking facilities used and required currency to finance agricultural production and to service small-scale mercantile transactions. The maldistribution was corrected to some degree

[10] *New York Tribune*, January 12, 1875.
[11] C. Vann Woodward, *Reunion and Reaction, The Compromise of 1877 and the End of Reconstruction* (Boston: Little, Brown, 1951), p. 149.

between 1865 and 1874 over the consistent opposition of New York representatives fearful of inflation.[12]

New York congressmen also voted against the Resumption Act of 1875 which ended the debate over the distribution of bank currency by establishing "free banking." The new system did not really serve the needs of the South because it linked the currency to United States bonds at a time when the national debt was declining in size and rising in value. New York vigorously resisted efforts to alter further the basis of bank note circulation or to inflate the currency. The city's desire for national security and uniformity fell most heavily on other—and poorer—people's shoulders. New York's insistence that the South "go it alone" helped to inhibit a fundamental restructuring of the Southern economy, accentuated regional differences and discouraged economic growth. New Yorkers, such as William Dodge, assumed that the promotion of transportation, the exploitation of natural resources and the development of manufacturing were the principal requisites of Southern prosperity. They ignored the more fundamental requirements of education, agricultural finance and improvement, and the diffusion of a general sense of participation in the rewards of society. The industrial enterprises ardently promoted in the 1880's, remained tiny outposts in a land of agricultural poverty.[13]

Decentralization, with many of the same implications for the transfer of resources from rich to poor, was the basic framework of local government and politics in New York. "It occurred to us," James Parton wrote in 1866, "that perhaps the best way of beginning an investigation of the city government would be to go down to the City Hall and look at it. It proved not to be there. To keep the whole city from falling a prey to the monster, it has been gradually cut to pieces, and scattered over the island. . . ." Parton breathlessly summarized the anatomy of fragmentation:

The Mayor has been deprived of all controlling power. The Board of Aldermen, seventeen in number, the Board of twenty-four Councilmen, the twelve Supervisors, the twenty-one members of the Board of Edu-

[12] Fritz Redlich, *The Molding of American Banking, Men and Ideas, Part II, 1840–1910* (New York: Hafner, 1951), pp. 118–121.
[13] C. Vann Woodward, *Origins of the New South*, History of the South (Baton Rouge: Louisiana University Press, 1951), pp. 139–141.

cation, are so many independent legislative bodies, elected by the people. The police are governed by four Commissioners, appointed by the Governor for eight years. The charitable and reformatory institutions of the city are in charge of four Commissioners whom the City Comptroller appoints for five years. The Commissioners of the Central Park, eight in number, are appointed by the Governor for five years. Four Commissioners, appointed by the Governor for eight years, manage the Fire Department. There are also five Commissioners of Pilots, two appointed by the Board of Underwriters and three by the Chamber of Commerce. The finances of the city are in charge of the Comptroller, whom the *people* elect for four years. The street department has at its head one Commissioner, who is appointed by the Mayor for four years. Three Commissioners, appointed by the Mayor, manage the Croton Aqueduct department. The law officer of the city, called the Corporation Counsel is elected by the *people* for three years! Six Commissioners, appointed by the Governor for six years, attend to the emigration from foreign countries To these has been recently added a Board of Health, the members of which are appointed by the Governor.

"Was there ever," Parton concluded, "such a hodgepodge of a government before in the world?" [14]

Parton might wisely have added an element of geography to his picture of decentralization. The history of the police force, for example, illustrates the influence of spatial distance upon the distribution of power. During the 1830's and 1840's, individual crime and persistent mob rioting demonstrated that the night watch and part-time constabulary could not protect life and property against violence. The state legislature in 1844 created a professional city police force of 800 men. The chief of police was selected by the mayor, but each of the members of his force was appointed annually upon the nomination of his ward councilmen. Each district captain, in cooperation with the politicians who had appointed him, was law in his own district. [15]

Each reorganization of the force which attempted to break the hold of this localism ultimately failed. The police could not

[14] James Parton, "The Government of the City of New York," *North American Review*, CII (1866), pp. 455–456.
[15] There is a brief sketch of police developments in Raymond Fosdick, *American Police Systems* (New York: Century, 1920), pp. 76–90.

draw on a class of administrators with a tradition of disinterested action in the public behalf. Americans found it difficult to believe that such action was even possible. Bipartisanship, rather than nonpartisanship, was understood as the principal guardian of the public interest. The introduction of party conflict into the internal structure of administrative organizations preserved liberty, as one element in the public interest, at the expense of the most elementary effectiveness in controlling crime. The ambitious attempt of the Republican-dominated state government in 1857 to control and restructure the city police force quickly disintegrated. Republicans and Democrats negotiated a gentlemen's agreement in 1864 to divide the police board between them. The agreement was continued after 1870 when the board was returned to solely municipal hands. Police administration was continually disrupted by party conflicts. The board could not control the corps. The captains were able without much interference to select the laws which were enforceable in their little kingdoms.[16]

There was a fundamental ambivalence in the social mandate for police action. The police were told, on the one hand, to wipe out gambling, prostitution, and disreputable concert saloons. They were urged, on the other, simply to isolate socially unacceptable behavior in the poorer sections, to drive the outcasts from the main thoroughfares. "Banish the Roughs," a *Tribune* headline trumpeted. "Concert Saloons and Gambling Cells Must Be Driven to the Slums." [17]

With an ambiguous mandate and an enormously difficult task, the police force was dispirited and open to political manipulation. The influence of the parties, in turn, made the task of effective police action even more difficult. The faults of the New York police force were opened to public view in the 1895 hearings of the Lexow Commission. The pattern revealed at the end of the century was already apparent in the seventies. A legislative committee under Thomas Cooper Campbell described the demorali-

[16] "Report of the Select Committee Appointed by the Assembly of 1875 to Investigate the Causes of the Increase of Crime in the City of New York, New York," *New York Assembly Documents,* 106th session, 1876 (Albany, 1876), VI, p. 5.
[17] *New York Tribune,* November 20, 1872.

zation of the force.[18] There were, first of all, too few policemen. The average night tour of duty extended over nearly a mile and a quarter; the day tour, over two miles. The average overworked patrolman found it difficult under these conditions to believe that the authorities really intended to enforce the law.

An informal "system" of police organization replaced the formal rules defined in the commissioners' manual. Appointments, promotions, and even tours of duty were secured through political influence. A dual system of central and precinct detectives engendered conflicts of authority which absorbed the energies of members of the force. Within their precincts, the captains were absolute monarchs, preying on both the criminals and the poorer classes "even when not criminals." The incentives to act effectively to fulfill the formal goals of the police force were systematically denied. Vigorous enforcement of the law would often prevent the promotion of a new officer. Arrests and indictments rarely led to convictions, discouraging even the most conscientious officers. There was, moreover, very little at stake in promotion within the regular organization. A rookie, after a month of schooling, made as much as the most experienced patrolman or roundsman (corporal). Promotion within the informal police "system," leading to a more lucrative tour of duty, was very desirable. It paid to go along.

Police commissioners were virtually powerless before the vested influence of the captains. An officer could only be dismissed after a departmental trial. It was difficult to obtain proper evidence from prostitutes and gamblers who had to continue to live in the district. The commissioners reassigned all captains to new posts in 1874 but the old patterns were quickly re-established.

Campbell's committee made several suggestions to strengthen the hand of the Police Board and to improve the morale of the force. The committee proposed doubling the size of the force and creating a single, select detective corps. The commissioners should be empowered to dismiss officers summarily and to develop a system of promotion on the basis of merit and graded pay. The committee also cut through the web of social demands which frustrated police efforts. "Houses of prostitution," they argued,

[18] This is the select committee whose report is cited in footnote 16.

"doubtless must exist and will continue to exist, whatever laws legislatures may pass, or whatever steps to enforce such laws police authorities may take." Would it not be better for the legislature to accept that fact and pass laws "not such as would be in accordance with the highest code or morals, but such as would enable the world to be the best governed and the greatest amount of happiness to accrue to the greatest number of persons?" Was it better to "nominally secure and then, in fact, allow a violation" of law, or to admit the inevitable and, through a licensing system, offer a real hope of control.[19]

The force was not doubled; a prostitution bill was not introduced. The police commissioners pressed for increased authority. Complicated by the issue of patrolmen's salaries, their measure did not pass. The political history of the Police Department during the decade never rose above the level of contention about the character, ability, or political persuasion of the commissioners themselves. Each of New York's mayors during the seventies was involved in acrimonious debate with the police board and attempted to remove the commissioners. The battles were tempests in teapots, distracting attention from the basic problems of law enforcement. They perpetuated, while seeming to debate, old patterns. Decentralized government reconciled law and opinion close to home.

Other agencies were subject to the same geographic fragmentation. Local trustees, rather than the central Board of Education, chose textbooks, selected teachers, and undertook school contracts. Local party leaders demanded and usually received consideration in the operations of governmental agencies within their districts. Even the Central Park Commission, which prided itself on its stable work force and policy of regular promotion on the basis of merit, distributed work tickets to the aldermen. The aldermen gave the tickets to laborers in their districts who, as a political favor, received jobs when they were available.[20]

Decentralization was written into almost every government

[19] *Ibid.*, pp. 22–34.
[20] Testimony of Henry Stebbins and William Martin, December 7, 1876, reported in the "Stenographic Minutes of Hearing Before the Mayor in the Matter of Charges Against Commissioners Martin and O'Donohue," Mayors Papers, Box 347.

function. The land of Manhattan was privately owned. Official street "openings" and the purchase of land were directed by special commissioners appointed by the Supreme Court for each particular task. The improvements were financed by local assessments on the property owners immediately benefited by the new roads. In 1846, the state constitutional convention had debated the policy of special assessments and rejected the argument that streets should be financed from the general treasury. The system of assessments and special commissioners allowed property owners more or less to determine the pace of street improvements. The citizenry directly established and paid for city decisions.[21]

Many government officers acted as political entrepreneurs, selling their services directly to the public. Entrepreneurship over and beyond the law gave New York an unenviable reputation for corruption. Entrepreneurship was, however, written into the law itself as the complement of the conception of public action for limited private benefit. Those who received services should pay for them. Coroners, the county sheriff, the minor judiciary, recorder and court clerks were all recompensed by direct fees. The Chamberlain assumed responsibility for the safety of public funds and, in return, was allowed to keep the interest on city bank deposits in his pocket.

The most characteristic response to the ineptitude of city government was to ask the state legislature to make the most significant local decisions. City tax rates, borrowing powers, salaries, building rules, and welfare expenditures were all formally determined in Albany. The legislators acted under conditions of extreme uncertainty. They had even less information about municipal affairs than the men at City Hall. The results of their policies only slowly "fed back" to Albany. Investigating committees, the legislative instruments of inspection and control, were clumsy and irregular. The criteria distinguishing "right" or "wise" policy from wrong and unwise were not very clear. The legislature was therefore readily open to persuasion by men who could form a coalition to pass a measure by paying for cooperation. Under these conditions, legislative decisions frequently appeared to be arbi-

[21] Victor Rosewater, *Special Assessments* (New York: Columbia University Press, 1893), pp. 27–28.

trary, autocratic, corrupt, and uninformed. Simple technical errors in the law were common.[22]

One basic decision, made at a distance in the state legislature and based upon an overly simple analysis of urban change, had a very decisive impact upon city politics. Left to itself, New York would probably have adopted a permissive policy to remove the "liquor question" from politics. Upstaters, who seemed to conceive of drink as the source of urban vice, blocked this alternative. The basic response of the city government to restrictive legislation was to allow lax administration. Periodic reform movements and the divided interests of liquor sellers, however, prevented a stable reconciliation of the legislative mandate with popular desires.

The instability which the liquor issue imposed upon city affairs was apparent in a characteristic episode of administrative history. The police commissioners in the spring of 1876 were engaged in one of their periodic attempts to assert their authority over the corps. They tried two captains for failure to enforce the Excise Law in their districts. The corps of captains, in order to embarrass their superiors, launched a citywide drive against Sunday liquor sales. Five hundred arrests were made on Sunday, May 21, touching both large and small establishments. The liquor dealers were outraged and the mayor expressed his displeasure. The aldermen resolved that enforcement of the law should not go beyond outward appearances. Policemen who entered the side door of a "closed" saloon, the aldermen stormed, were making the Sabbath "hideous by their rude and unlawful intrusion." The police commissioners did not quite know what to do. The resolved that the Superintendent, the professional head of the force, should not issue an order for the general enforcement of any statute without consulting them, but he should, of course, not hesitate to enforce "all laws now in force." [23]

The police captains, proving their point, generated more changes than they knew or intended. They demonstrated that enforcement of the Sunday prohibition was possible, and em-

---

[22] Willard Hurst comments in a similar vein on the general inexperience of state legislators. *The Growth of American Law: The Law Makers* (Boston: Little, Brown, 1950), pp. 49–50.

[23] *New York Tribune*, May 22, 26, 27, 1876.

boldened temperance committees to demand continued exertions. The Excise Board promised its cooperation in the effort to restrict unlicensed dealers. Its promise was quickly put to the test by a surprising judicial decision. The Court of Appeals ruled in April, 1877, that the board could not license retail liquor dealers to sell anything but ale or beer. Only hotels or taverns providing at least three beds for overnight guests could be licensed to sell spirits.

The dealers were alarmed at the sweeping threat to their business. The board was at a loss for a policy. While it promised not to be satisfied with a merely technical compliance with the law it did not feel ready to rescind licenses already granted. The board contested charges that it allowed vast numbers of unlicensed groggeries. Its task was simply to issue the licenses, and not to enforce the law. The courts, jammed by mass arrests, faced an almost impossible task. One judge complained that he was being asked to do a job which had required the federal militia in other states. A grand jury in December, 1877, declared the excise system a "public scandal." Saloons became hotels by placing three beds in a corner or in an upstairs room. Dealers who could not get liquor permits accepted licenses for beer and ale, and then continued to sell spirits. The liquor dealers, on their side, protested that enforcement was too vigorous, that a legitimate business interest was being "persecuted." [24]

All attempts to change the law failed and a pattern of neglect, sporadic enforcement, and nagging corruption was firmly established. Society made its adjustment to the imposition of a uniform policy upon a divided city.

As the complaining judge attested, decentralization and the confused lines of authority and responsibility placed a heavy burden on the courts. They were frequently asked to judge whether a decision had been made in the proper form by the appropriate officer or agency. They became, in effect, arbiters of management procedures. They were hardly equipped for this function. They were organized to allow successive and costly appeals. After extensive hearings and countless forms (all of which had to be precisely correct in their wordings), the decisions of the street commissioners, for example, were open freely to extensive appeals

[24] *New York Tribune*, August 18, 1877; December 8, 1877.

and revisions by the courts. The system was so riddled with legal technicalities, and so open to both honest mistakes and corrupt manipulation, that the courts were as likely to vacate a contested assessment as to sustain it.[25] Prior to 1870, Justices of the New York Supreme Court, the highest trial bench in the state, had overlapping jurisdictions and could negate each other's orders. In 1867, Jay Gould and Cornelius Vanderbilt, fighting for control of the Erie Railroad, traded injunctions and counter-injunctions wrung from compliant judges in New York City and Binghamton.[26]

Political parties supplied the major element of political coordination in New York in the 1860's and 1870's. The city, divided by a primitive communications network, had only a limited toleration for coordination and the powers of the party hierarchy were severely limited. The term "boss" applied to William Marcy Tweed or to John Kelly, his successor, is a measure of the mystery which surrounded their activities, not of their political omnipotence. Each city district had a central Democratic and Republican party committee with a great deal of autonomy in its local affairs and in the nomination of district aldermen, assemblymen, state senators, and congressmen. The central leadership rested uneasily on top of this local structure. Tweed's pre-eminence in city politics began in 1866 but was not confirmed by victory in Albany until the election of 1869. Tweed's control was seriously challenged in 1870 by discontented local politicians, and he was beaten in 1871. The candidates endorsed by "Honest" John Kelly, were defeated at the polls in 1872, 1875 and 1878. Kelly himself was virtually forced out of the regular Democratic party.

There was only one way New York could be "bossed" in the 1860's. The lines of communication were too narrow, the patterns of deference too weak, to support freely acknowledged and stable leadership. Only a universal payment of benefits—a giant "pay-off" —could pull the city together in a common effort. The only treasury big enough to support coordination was the public till.

[25] *New York Tribune*, November 18, 1872.
[26] The classic account is Charles Francis Adams, Jr. and Henry Adams, *Chapters of Erie and Other Essays* (New York: Henry Holt, 1886).

SEVEN

The Moment of Opportunity

For a moment, at the end of the 1860's and the beginning of the 1870's, it appeared that New York's governmental institutions would be reconstructed and a comprehensive attack would be launched on all of the myriad disabilities of urban life. The waterfront, the business districts, the tenement houses, and the new areas of the upper city cried for relief.

The movement of population northward, temporarily halted by the war, began again with the close of hostilities. The simple gridiron street plan of 1811 seriously limited expansion into the hilly areas on the West Side of Manhattan above 59th Street. Prior to the war, a few attempts had been made to cut straight streets through mountains of rocks, but they had almost all been abandoned. A few narrow roads strung the houses out along the edges of precipices or deep in canyons. The main lines of traffic anticipated by the original commissioners lay east and west, not north and south. Construction along the original lines would, therefore, have substantially isolated the new section from the older settlement.[1]

The Central Park Commission was entrusted by the legislature with the major tasks of redesigning the West Side. The commissioners were engagingly frank in discussing the constraints under which they acted. Their reports reveal the difficulties of thorough reconstruction, even in a largely uninhabited region. Nineteenth century Americans showed very little concern for vested rights

---

[1] Board of Commissioners of the Central Park, *Eleventh Annual Report, For the Year Ending with December 31, 1863* (New York, 1868), p. 134.

when they inhibited individual liberty. Masters were not compensated for the loss of their slaves; husbands for the loss of the rights to their wives' property; the Charles River Bridge Company for the collapse of its monopoly.[2] At the same time, vested rights which protected individual liberty against a vaguely defined public or community interest were deeply cherished. The Central Park Commission repeatedly insisted on its respect for the established pattern of land ownership and individual initiative.

The commission was empowered to change the plan of the West Side between 59th and 155th streets and to design anew the most northern sections of the island. It proposed to make only modest changes in the customary gridiron. "In dealing with such an extent of territory so much subdivided," the commissioners explained in 1867, they thought it best to confine their efforts to removing the chief obstacles to individual improvement. They discontinued overly steep grades and abandoned the attempt to drive public roads up the precipitous slopes along the Hudson and Harlem rivers. They planned a series of north-south avenues conforming as closely as possible to existing roads and realigned the shoreline. Two considerations, they confessed, dictated against designing "new streets, avenues, squares, parks, and terraces," and led them to "forebare interference with existing lines of streets and avenues except where obvious advantages were to be reached." The first was expense and the second was the "injury to existing subdivisions of property" which would be left "in unfit parcels to build upon, except by the tedious processes of exchange and sales between owners."[3]

Andrew Green, the comptroller and dominant figure on the commission, explained its problems in detail. The land on the West Side between 55th and 155th streets, although largely uninhabited, had already been subdivided into 332 blocks, each originally carved into 64 lots measuring 25 by 100 feet. He prepared a list

[2] Willard Hurst, *Law and the Conditions of Freedom in the Nineteenth Century United States* (Madison: University of Wisconsin Press, 1956), pp. 23–29.
[3] Board of Commissioners of the Central Park, *Eleventh Annual Report, op. cit.*, pp. 74–75.

to demonstrate that it was not the demands of a few wealthy men which confined the commission's endeavors:

49 of the blocks were owned by a single individual
104 of the blocks were divided among 2–5 owners
101 of the blocks were divided among 5–10 owners
63 of the blocks were divided among 10–20 owners
12 of the blocks were divided among 20–30 owners
3 of the blocks were divided among 30–40 owners
1 of the blocks was divided among 50 owners

A few large institutions, notably Trinity Church and Leake and Watts Children's Home owned large tracts of land, but there were several thousand owners of property in the area in addition to the institutions. Since each lot, Green contended, was entitled by law to access to a public street, and land for nearly half the necessary streets had already been acquired by the city prior to the war, the only measure likely to meet public favor was the construction of broad longitudinal avenues.[4]

This planning left its mark on the later social organization of the West Side. The construction of a few great thoroughfares necessitated lengthening the intersecting streets. Long blocks with fewer open corners proved to be not quite as safe as short blocks. They lacked visual coherence and made it more difficult for neighbors to develop a feeling of mutual concern for their common interests and problems.[5]

The restrictions which Green accepted upon his ability to redesign the area were severe. The size of the standard lot was not changed and no new provision was made for frequent squares. Green specifically excluded as too expensive the possibility of merging blocks and planning homes facing a central green. He denied, for similar reasons, the possibility of creating pedestrian lanes closed to vehicles between rows of houses.[6]

[4] *Ibid.*, pp. 134–137.
[5] The Importance of short blocks is a central theme in Jane Jacobs, *The Death and Life of Great American Cities* (New York: Random House, 1961). See particularly pp. 178–186.
[6] Board of Commissioners of the Central Park, *Eleventh Annual Report, op. cit.*, pp. 135–140.

Within the limits he accepted, Green acted with an intense concern for orderly development. The execution of any plan, he pointed out, would require enormous sums of money. The faults of a poorly considered plan would have to be remedied in the future at additional expense. "We need not go off our own island," he argued, "to see lamentable results of the want of largeness of ideas in the attempts that have been made to provide for the wants of a great people." He laid down a series of guide lines. Sewers and drains must be planned and constructed before streets. Cheap pavements needing constant repair would soon prove to be more expensive than pavements properly laid. The streets should be wide enough to allow the free movement of traffic but not so wide as to raise costs prohibitively. Provisions should be made in advance for the unfortunate, but probably inevitable, construction of street railroads. Owners of adjoining property should be prevented from encroaching upon the public way. Adequate recreational facilities should be prepared, lest a green and airy countryside be turned rapidly, and unthinkingly, into a city without open spaces.

Green's plans included a newly broadened Sixth, Seventh, and Eighth Avenue, a boulevard running from 155th Street to 59th Street and Eighth Avenue, and two parks with accompanying drives at Morningside and Riverside. He cautioned against a mad rush to actually build every street and park laid out on his map. "It would be unwise," he wrote, "to exercise the power of opening and working streets before they are needed; the owners interested should not be required to advance the moneys to pay the necessary expenses, long before a compensating use can be made of the property." It was vitally important, however, to define and fix a plan to which private builders could accommodate themselves.[7]

Efforts comparable to those launched on the West Side were also undertaken on the waterfront. New York's twenty-mile shore-

[7] Andrew H. Green, *Communication to the Commissioners of the Central Park Relative to the Improvement of the Sixth and Seventh Avenues, From the Central Park to the Harlem River; the Laying Out of the Island Above 155th Street, the Drive from 59th Street to 155th Street, and Other Subjects* (New York, 1866), pp. 1–2, 8–9, 31–35, 38–40, 53–55, 73–75.

line housed 155 wharves in 1870. Sixty-four were publicly owned. The city had a share in 34 and the remainder were owned and managed by private parties. Built at different angles and irregular intervals they wasted space in the crowded lower city. Harbor officials, surveying the docks in 1864, described only ten as in "good" or "fair" order; the balance were in varying stages of disrepair or absolute decay. While private mercantile building, they noted, had pioneered in modern forms and conveniences, the public docks were old and obsolete. The bulkhead walls which lined the shore were a cheap cribwork, requiring frequent repair. Reeking sewage clung to the undersides of the bulkhead and docks.[8]

The expansion of dock facilities uptown along the Hudson was inhibited by the confusion of authority. The legislature in 1837 gave the city control over the underwater land of the shoreline west of Twelfth Avenue. These lands and rights were quickly granted to private owners. Squabbles over the waterfront led to the fixing of a new legal shoreline in 1857. The line was drawn inland so that there was no water at the projected bulkhead. Neither the city nor private parties were empowered to excavate so that the real water could reach the legal shore.[9]

A committee of the Citizens Association, including some of the leading steamship owners in the city, recommended in 1867 that the city lease the public piers to private capitalists on the condition that they rebuild them. Steamship companies requiring permanent and extensive dock facilities should be granted special locations. Many owners of domestic sailing vessels and Hudson River barges were unhappy with this proposal. They feared that they would lose prime waterfront locations. The legislation which emerged from these conflicting interests in 1870 gave a new Department of Docks control of the waterfront. The department was

[8] Department of Docks, *Public Meetings to Hear Persons Interested in Improving the River Front, June and July, 1870* (New York, 1870), pp. 7–11. Board of Health of the Health Department of the City of New York, *First Annual Report, April 11, 1870, to April 10, 1871* (New York, 1871), p. 15; Leveson Francis Vernon-Harcourt, *Harbours and Docks* (Oxford, 1885), I, p. 624.
[9] Board of Commissioners of the Central Park, *Eleventh Annual Report, op. cit.*, pp. 138–40.

required to develop a new system of docks for the sites already under the city's control, and to purchase new land. If regular negotiations failed, it was empowered to claim private property through condemnation proceedings under the right of eminent domain. It was also allowed to extend the bulkhead line into the harbor. To fulfill their program, the dock commissioners could borrow up to $3,000,000 each year.[10]

A representative of the Citizens Association, Judge Joseph A. Daly, addressed the first open session of the new department in June, 1870. Judge Daly lauded the Board of Dock Commissioners as a unique non-partisan endeavor clothed with a sweeping authority of the sort known in England. "The greatest work of reform yet inaugurated in our city," he concluded, "is now in the full tide of experiment." [11]

The city's attention was focused upon expansion. The building of badly needed sewers in old districts was delayed in favor of construction in largely uninhabited regions. "The board," sewer officials explained, "has thought it of superior consequence to first satisfy the necessities of the extraordinary growth of population rather than to divert its energy toward the correction of an evil which can be postponed with less injury to the citizens at large." [12] The movement of population out of the tenement districts, rather than fundamental changes in the old city, held the greatest promise of reform. Bridges across the Hudson and East rivers, a writer in the *Catholic World* insisted, would be as important as pure water and Central Park in relieving the "immense surplus of population, which it is impossible for us to accommodate in our midst." [13] John A. Roebling's plans for the Brooklyn Bridge were approved in 1869.[14]

Schemes for rapid transportation were rife. A demonstration

[10] Sub-Committee on Wharves and Piers of the Citizens Association, *Report: December 13, 1867* (New York, 1867); *Laws, 1870*, c. 383.

[11] Department of Docks, *Public Meetings: June and July, 1870*, p. 17.

[12] U. S. Census Office, *Tenth Census of the United States*, XVIII, "Report on the Social Statistics of Cities" (Washington, 1886), pp. 571–572.

[13] "The Sanitary and Moral Condition of New York City," *Catholic World*, VII (1868), p. 558.

[14] David B. Steinman, *The Builders of the Bridge* (New York: Harcourt, Brace, 1945), pp. 306–322.

section of a pneumatic subway was built by Alfred Beach in 1870 and a small car was "blown back and forth every day under Broadway." Beach could not get up enough wind to counteract the influence of the city's political leaders who backed an elevated line in which they had a personal financial interest.[15] After a troubled beginning, a line running along Greenwich Street and Ninth Avenue on the West Side got off the ground. By 1871 the El extended to 30th Street where passengers could transfer to the New York and Harlem. Two further branches of a Viaduct Railroad were projected to encircle Manhattan. The company was granted rights of eminent domain over private property and free use of the streets. After an initial private subscription, the city was to subscribe $5,000,000 to start construction.[16]

The older residential areas were not entirely neglected. In 1866 and 1867, the legal and institutional bases for public regulation of housing and health were substantially strengthened. A decade-long campaign against the dangers of the tenement was climaxed by fear of a city-wide cholera epidemic. The legislature rushed to create a Metropolitan Board of Health which quickly gained prestige in the spring of 1866 because the city was saved from the dreaded disease. The board was empowered to order any "building, erection, excavation, premises, business pursuit, matter or thing" to be "purified, cleaned, disinfected, altered or improved." It was given almost unlimited rights of entry and inspection. In its first rush of enterprise the board removed 160,000 tons of manure from vacant lots and issued more than thirty thousand special orders. The city smelled just a little bit better.[17]

The board in 1870 promised to use its power to reorganize the physical and hence the social structure of the slums so that they could share the dominant values of American society. The commissioners promised to encourage "the greatest possible isolation

[15] Robert Daly, "Alfred Ely Beach and His Wonderful Pneumatic Underground Railway," *American Heritage*, CII, 4 (June, 1961), pp. 54–57, 85–89.

[16] *Laws, 1871*, c. 300; *American Railroad Journal*, Second Quarto Series, XXVII (1871), pp. 821–822.

[17] Charles Rosenberg, *The Cholera Years* (Chicago: University of Chicago Press, 1962), pp. 192–212.

and privacy for each individual and family as a means of promoting self-respect." [18]

The legislature in 1866 also approved a building act sponsored by the fire insurance companies, the soundest of the city's builders and the association of architects. The law, designed to prevent fire, required that plans for every building constructed in New York had to be approved by the municipal Building Department. Tenement houses were specifically regulated for the first time in 1867. The new law required landlords to make at least minimal provisions for ventilation, sanitation, and safety. The law established standards for the distance between buildings, the location of rear dwellings, and the sizes of rooms and windows. The department was empowered to close houses which were badly in need of repair.[19]

In the early stages of the movement for city improvement, the legislature responded to many different pressures. There was no central directorate which approved all bills, determined priorities or even set the costs of passage. Until the beginning of the session of 1870, Republicans enjoyed a majority in the legislature although they had lost the executive mansion in 1868. The creation of the metropolitan boards and the allocation of authority to the Central Park Commission were both designed to prevent New York Democrats from controlling the profits of expansion and improvement.

The victory of the Democrats in the state election of 1869 linked Albany to City Hall. The "moment of opportunity," became Tweed's moment. The drive towards improvement was captured, broadened, and finally damned. The history of Tweed's rise and fall, Kelly's ascendency and limitation, is a measure of the collapse of a broad-scale attack on the "problem" of the city. New York, divided and tamed overly-ambitious public entrepreneurs.

William Marcy Tweed, for all his bulk, is a man hidden in the shadows of Thomas Nast's leering cartoons in *Harpers Weekly*. The other members of his ring were real enough. A. Oakey Hall, Mayor from 1869 to 1872, covered a keen and, one suspects,

---

[18] Board of Health, *First Annual Report, op. cit.*, p. 50.
[19] *Laws, 1866*, c. 873; *1867*, c. 908.

brooding intelligence with an exterior mask at once a little too witty and a little too elegant. Peter Sweeny, Tweed's adviser and parks commissioner, was a well-trained lawyer of skill and sophistication. Under attack, he remained scornfully aggressive and contemptuous of his detractors. Richard Connolly, city comptroller, was an obsequious man. Fearful of being victimized by his friends, in the last days of the Tweed Ring he turned to his enemies for support and justification. Used and then spurned, he ended as a pitiful, if wealthy, object of contempt.[20]

The Boss himself is more difficult to characterize. In Nast's portraits, Tweed is a lecherous, corrupt, and powerful Falstaff. Bargaining for pardon in the later seventies, he displayed a softness which fit this image. Sweeny, he complained, was a "hard, over-bearing, revengeful man." [21] What is missing from the image is an explanation of Tweed's real personal powers, his ability to ingratiate himself with men of respectability and with low politicians, his breadth of political imagination and his vindictiveness. All one can say about Tweed is that he was predictable. He united the elements in a divided society in the only manner in which they could be united: by paying them off. Attracted to a scorned profession, he acted with scorn for conventional social ethics. Like so many American entrepreneurs, he maximized his short run profits and then got out.

Tweed's climb to political power was a classic American success story. Even his setbacks stood him in good stead. He rose through the ranks rapidly as leader of a local volunteer fire company, alderman, and then congressman. Two years in Washington bored him, but in 1854 he had the political good fortune to be defeated for reelection by a candidate of the nativist (Know-Nothing) American party. The badge of his defeat was helpful in a city soon to have a large Catholic voting population. After the election he accepted a post as commissioner in the Board of Education where his hand touched building and supply contracts. He was elected to the new Board of Supervisors of the County of New York in 1857. The board flourished on the profits real-

[20] Charles F. Wingate, "An Episode in Municipal Government," *North American Review*, CXIX (1874), pp. 368–371.
[21] *New York Herald*, October 10, 1877.

Thomas Nast on Tweed, 1871: The leaders were villains and the Irish followers were hardly human.
Historical Pictures Service—Chicago

ized from the painfully slow and costly construction of a new County Court House.[22]

The Democratic party in New York was severely divided from 1857 to 1865 by controversy growing out of the Civil War crisis. Democratic dissension allowed the election of a Republican mayor in 1861 and the victory of the candidate of a splinter Democratic faction two years later. At the end of the war unity was restored. Tammany Hall, led by Tweed and Sweeny, emerged as the dominant political organization in the city, hardly challenged by the remnants of rival groups and working closely with the national party leaders in New York. Tammany's candidate, John T. Hoffman, was elected mayor in 1866. The Democratic National Convention of 1868, which nominated former Governor Horatio Seymour to oppose Grant for the presidency, was held in Tammany's resplendent new building, finished just in time to accommodate the delegates. In the fall, Tweed gave the voters a considerable hand in carrying New York for Seymour. Hoffman was elected governor and was replaced by Hall in the mayor's office. The Democracy captured the state legislature for the first time in twenty years in the election of 1869.[23]

Tweed was a master of the strategy of the leadership which succeeds because it allows men to do as they please. The Board of Education allowed teachers in predominately Catholic neighborhoods to put aside the little Protestant rituals of the American public school. The police and excise boards smiled on both the men who filled the cups and the imbibers. The Sabbath could be enjoyed in New York with drink in hand despite a state law which prohibited the sale of liquor on Sunday.[24]

[22] Wingate, "An Episode in Municipal Government," *North American Review*, CXIX (1874), pp. 361–368.

[23] The standard political histories of this period are: Stewart Mitchell, *Horatio Seymour* (Cambridge: Harvard University Press, 1938); Alexander C. Flick and G. S. Lobrano, *Samuel Jones Tilden* (New York: Dodd, Mead, 1939), the third volume of De Alva Stanwood Alexander, *A Political History of the State of New York* (New York: Henry Holt, 1909); and Homer A. Stebbins, *Political History of New York, 1865–1869* (New York: Columbia University Press, 1939).

[24] The rabid anti-Catholicism of *Harpers Weekly* was fed on the city's educational and excise policy. See Thomas Nast's cartoon, "The American River Ganges," XV (September 30, 1871), p. 916.

Tweed was a master communicator. With massive sums of money at his disposal, he united the fragmented news media. Several reporters on each paper received stipends from city officials to ensure favorable coverage. Public advertising supported both the largest newspapers and the host of tiny journals smiling favorably at the Boss. "Bought" stories in out-of-town papers were reprinted in New York and "created the impression that the entire nation admired the city government." [25]

More positively, and with a fresher hand, Tweed rallied diverse groups behind his programs. He encouraged Catholic allegiance to the Democracy by a policy of state and city aid to parochial schools and private charities. The Church received nearly $1,500,000 from public sources between 1869 and 1871. Labor unions were encouraged to organize and allowed to strike.[26] Tweed energetically promoted the development program and the reorganization of the city government. His policies won support in high and respectable circles. His implicit motto was "something for everyone." His tactical plan was "do it now." Andrew Green and the Central Park Commission argued for restrained growth and a careful regard for costs; Tweed and his associates, for unlimited expansion and far-ranging public expenditures.

The system of special assessments on property owners benefited by improvements was a major obstacle to large-scale development. Mayor Hall in April, 1869 ridiculed the idea that city improvements could be financed through assessments and attacked the "rich old men who cannot realize that New York is no longer a series of straggling villages." In the following month the legislature permitted the city to pay up to one-half the costs of street opening and improvement above 14th Street and the entire cost below 14th Street from the general treasury.[27] This was an important change both for business and residential streets. Tenement house owners were frequently unwilling or unable to repave the streets which adjoined their property.

[25] Morris Weiner, *Tammany Hall* (New York: Doubleday, 1928), pp. 206–207.
[26] *Laws, 1870*, c. 19; *1871*, c. 875. John W. Pratt, "Boss Tweed's Public Welfare Program," *New York Historical Society Quarterly*, XLV, 4 (October, 1961), pp. 396–411 adopts a similar view of Tweed.
[27] *New York Times*, April 29, 1869; *Laws, 1869*, c. 890.

Authorization for new—and needed—public programs poured from the legislative halls. With several more limited alternatives available, the legislature, under Tweed's prodding, chose a sweeping program for the docks. The dock commissioners approved a design prepared by General George C. McClellan for broad waterfront avenues, a masonry bulkhead around the lower island, and a system of uniform piers, including two to be built of stone. The first step suggested by McClellan was repurchasing land which the city had previously alienated. The city was also given virtually free and unlimited borrowing powers to improve the sewerage system, water supply, bridges in the northern city, and streets. Householders were encouraged to make repairs. The city would cover the expenses of ripping up the pavement adjoining a house and could be repaid over a period of five years.[28]

Democrats had long protested the absence of home rule. The need for governmental coordination of expanding activities allied them with groups of normally hostile businessmen anxious to bring order and efficiency out of chaos. Mayor Hall in his annual message in January, 1870 pointed out the anomalies of city government. Three different sets of officials controlled the streets. Each of the major departments presented an independent budget to the legislature and controlled its own expenditures. The metropolitan police were legally independent of local ordinances and supervision. The mayor was a figurehead unable to control his subordinates.[29]

The passage of a new charter in 1870, which Tweed admitted cost him at least $600,000, did not entirely cut through this tangle but it did promise to simplify city government and to centralize responsibility. The commissions were abolished and city departments were established in their place. The mayor's control remained marginal but he was allowed at least to appoint the department heads. The major beneficiary of the concentration of authority was Tweed, as superintendent of public works. The

[28] *Laws, 1871*, chaps. 290, 218, 56. Provisions for expanding activity and borrowing are scattered through a host of other measures in 1870 and 1871.
[29] Mayor of the City of New York, *Message to the Common Council, January 3, 1870* (New York, 1870).

greater part of the city development projects, including responsibility for uptown streets, which had previously belonged to the Central Park Commission, was placed in his hands. The superintendent was appointed for a term of four years and could be removed from office only after a trial before the Court of Common Pleas.[30]

The charter promised financial order where there was only chaos. A special Board of Audit was created to close the affairs of the redundant county offices. The board was authorized to audit the liabilities of the county and to issue, in payment, revenue bonds redeemable from the tax levy of 1871. A consolidated bond was also approved. Municipal finances were still largely directed at Albany, but the city gained greater control over its own taxes and debt than it had ever enjoyed before. Samuel Jones Tilden, chairman of the New York State Democratic Committee, denounced the proposed charter as a scheme of despotic government foreign to the American system. The old philanthropist Peter Cooper, for the Citizen's Association, on the other hand, lauded the charter as it was being debated in the legislature. After its passage, the membership of the association endorsed the document. The endorsement was signed by a long list of prominent New Yorkers led by James Brown, the venerable head of the most esteemed private banking firm in the city, and John Jacob Astor, probably the largest private owner of real estate in New York.[31]

At every step, Tweed associated his ambitious political program with his own personal interests. He indulged in a pattern of multiple office holding which would have warmed the heart of an eighteenth century placeman. He was at one and the same time superintendent of public works, county supervisor, state senator, Grand Sachem of the Tammany Society, chairman of the Democratic-Republican General Committee of the City of New York (Tammany Hall), and supervisor of the County Court

[30] *Laws, 1870*, c. 366.

[31] John Bigelow, ed., *The Writings and Speeches of Samuel J. Tilden* (New York: Duell, Harper, 1885), I, p. 568; Edward C. Mack, *Peter Cooper, Citizen of New York* (New York: Duell, Harper, 1949), pp. 350–354; Citizens Association of New York, *Address to the People of the City of New York* (New York, 1870).

House. Together with his friends and relatives, he speculated extensively in city real estate.

The city Boss joined hands with the arch speculators and business titans of his day. Jay Gould engaged Tweed's aid during the great battle with Cornelius Vanderbilt of the New York Central for control of the Erie Railroad in 1868. The Boss used his influence with New York judges and secured the passage of a law altering the method of electing Erie's board of directors in Gould's favor. Judge Albert Cardoza, one of Tweed's faithful legion, protected Gould in 1869 from paying his debts after an unsuccessful attempt to corner the gold market. The Erie received special privileges in the transportation of westward-bound immigrants from the reception center at Castle Garden. Tweed, in return, was elected to the Erie board and received Gould's political aid in the counties along the railroad's route.[32]

Tweed was not sparing with his gifts. With the titans at peace, he served as Vanderbilt's legislative representative in Albany. The owners of land on the East Side pressed the city in 1871 to force Vanderbilt's New York and Harlem River Railroad to cover its tracks along Fourth Avenue. The Commodore, with Tweed's support, consented only to sink the tracks below the street level and successfully demanded that the city pay half the cost of improvement.[33]

The Central Park Commission, reorganized as a Parks Department, was an important prize in Tweed's battle to control the city. The park system became a tool for political manipulation. Green remained on the board but was stripped of his executive powers. These were shared by Sweeny as president and by Henry Hilton as vice-president and treasurer. Hilton was the legal counsel and business associate of A. T. Stewart, the largest dry-goods merchant in the city. Old employees were dismissed and the work force was enlarged, probably, as Green contended,

---

[32] Julius Grodinsky, *Jay Gould, His Business Career, 1867–1892* (Philadelphia: University of Pennsylvania Press, 1957), pp. 47, 71, 79, *New York Times,* June 28, 1871; Matthew W. Breen, *Thirty Years of New York Politics, Up-to-Date* (New York, 1899), pp. 143–144.

[33] *New York Herald,* October 10, 1877; *Laws, 1871,* c. 225; *New York Tribune,* December 13, 15, 19, 20, 30, 1871.

to provide for political favorites. The board established handsome administrative quarters for itself.[34]

At the same time that they exploited the patronage of the Parks Department, the new commissioners attempted serious changes in policy. They granted private amusement and refreshment concessions in Central Park. Several alterations were made in the basic plan of the park, designed to facilitate movement and to provide for more formal recreational areas. The changes in and of themselves, Frederick Law Olmsted, the park's original designer, later admitted, were not necessarily deleterious but they violated his unified conception of structure and landscape and intruded upon his attempt to relieve dreary "urban conditions" by providing open and natural vistas. The changes projected the city into the park.[35]

In addition to changing the design of Central Park, the new commissioners shifted funds from the giant park to speed improvement of small parks and squares downtown. This shift represented a change in the distribution of benefits between social groups and also reflected a respect for the possibility of distinctly urban forms of excitement and recreation. Olmsted, assuming that the urban environment was inevitably dreary, attempted to relieve the monotony by a greenbelt of parks which would bring the country into the city. He envisioned his parks as community centers which would bring "closely together, poor and rich, young and old, Jew and Gentile" in a "social, neighborly, unexertive form of recreation." He insisted that the parks should present a sharp contrast to the "restraining and confining conditions of the town . . . which compel us to walk circumspectly, watchfully, jealously, . . . to look closely upon others without sympathy." [36]

Olmsted's imagination leaped to a vision of the city as a united community. Practically, since movement was difficult and costly, his park for all became a park for the better half of society.

[34] Board of Commissioners of the Department of Public Parks, *First Annual Report for the Year Ending May 1, 1871* (New York, 1871), pp. 5, 26.
[35] Board of Commissioners of Public Parks, *Second Annual Report for the Year Ending May 1, 1872* (New York, 1872), pp. 70–80.
[36] Board of Commissioners of the Department of Public Parks, *First Annual Report*, p. 46; Frederick Law Olmsted, "Public Parks and the Enlargement of Towns," *Journal of Social Science, III* (1870), pp. 18, 20.

The Parks Department, with a narrower and more fragmented image, focused on smaller urban neighborhood centers. Sweeny could not afford to share Olmsted's scorn for the "young men in knots of perhaps half a dozen in lounging attitudes rudely obstructing the sidewalks" or descending into a "brilliantly lighted basement, where they find others of their sort, see, hear, smell, drink, and eat all manner of vile things." [37]   The public square extended the sidewalk and basement rather than refuting them.

Finally, Tweed made the public treasury his own. Just as he paid others, he charged the city handsomely for his services. Every city contractor padded his bills to finance a "rake-off" for the Boss and his friends. In this thievery, Tweed was undone, the "moment of opportunity" spent, and the costs of urban coordination through a giant "pay-off" revealed.

[37] Olmsted, "Public Parks and the Enlargement of Towns," *Journal of Social Science,* III (1870), pp. 20, 21.

EIGHT

The Fall of the Ring

The story of Tweed's fall in 1871 is a study in the negative exercise of power. The men who could depose the king, could not ascend the throne themselves and lead.

Frederick Law Olmsted, who lost his job with the accession of the new park commissioners, told a story in 1870 which illustrated the differences between a negative veto and positive leadership. Olmsted described a well-to-do gentleman who had criticized his plans for Central Park as overly elaborate. "Why," the critic complained, "I should not ask for anything finer in my private grounds for the use of my own family." "Possibly," Olmsted replied, "grounds might not unwisely be prepared even more carefully when designed for the use of two hundred thousand families, than when designed for the use of one." The success of a park program for the general good, he continued, required the creation of an elite to whom the electorate could give charge of the parks, self-consciously attempting to free policy from the demands of special interests.[1]

It was obviously impossible in New York to build such an elite on the basis of scorn. Even with best of intentions, leaders would have difficulty guiding voters with whom they could not communicate. The elite could not lead if it doubted the worth of the public life. E. L. Godkin, editor of the *Nation*, echoed Olmsted's critic in the wake of Tweed's fall. "Men's great object in life," Godkin insisted, "is not to carry on government, but to follow their callings." Private occupations devoured the businessman's

[1] Frederick Law Olmsted, "Public Parks and the Enlargement of Towns," *Journal of Social Science*, III (1870), p. 29.

time. The railroad and telegraph had increased the pace of life so that it was impossible "for men to pay any fruitful attention to politics without neglecting their private affairs." [2] The reform commitment could only be the sporadic impluse of the outraged critic.

The outraged critics responded when their pocketbooks were threatened. The development of the city in the late sixties was financed largely by the issue of city bonds. The tax rate actually dropped between 1867 and 1871. Tweed successfully sponsored a bill in 1870 which provided that the rate should never exceed 2 per cent of the assessed value of property. Critics charged that the law was deceptive and, although the tax rate would be cut, assessments would be increased. They were wrong. Assessments did not rise unusually—the city debt did. The municipal indebtedness in 1867 was just short of $30,000,000; four years later it had reached nearly $90,000,000. Two thirds of the increase was contracted between January 1, 1869 and September 16, 1871. [3]

The largest part of the new bonds was placed with savings banks and trust companies which mushroomed after the war, largely unrestrained by governmental restrictions on their investments or by public inspection. The city did not attempt to raise funds through the national banks where extended borrowing might well have led to comment and resistance. By 1871 savings banks in the state held approximately 50 million dollars worth of city and county bonds. Several Tammany officials were bank officers. [4]

Additional bonds were placed with private bankers, particularly those selling to foreign investors. The New York, Frankfort, and Paris houses of the Seligman family underwrote $2,000,000 worth of city bonds at 72 per cent of their face value in 1869. The

---

[2] E. L. Godkin, "Rich Men in City Politics," *Nation*, XIII (November 16, 1871), pp. 316–317. Godkin's argument reinforces Richard Meier's conception of the usefulness of time budgets as measures of social change. *A Communications Theory of Urban Growth* (Cambridge: M.I.T. Press, 1962).

[3] Edward Durand, *The Finances of New York City* (New York: Macmillan, 1898), pp. 373, 375; Elmer Davis, *History of the New York Times, 1851–1921* (New York: New York Times, 1921), pp. 91–92.

[4] *Commercial and Financial Chronicle*, XII (November 25, 1871), pp. 686–687.

London and Frankfort branches of the House of Rothschild and the Discounts Gesellschaft in Berlin in April 1870 undertook a $3,000,000 issue which the Seligmans had refused.[5] The following year August Belmont, for the Rothschilds, bought outright $15,-000,000 worth of 6 per cent thirty-year gold bonds. The purchase was negotiated secretly for fear that knowledge of such a large issue would alarm the savings banks and other holders of municipal securities.[6]

The bond market was the Achilles Heel of the Tweed Ring. The city could enforce tax collections, but it could not coerce investors into purchasing securities. Impairment of the city's credit in foreign capital markets would hinder the efforts of city financiers to place other securities abroad.[7]

The burden of debt and the character of city expansion also directly affected the business of financiers handling real estate mortgages. The corporate holders of mortgages, although they were interested in development, were a peculiarly powerful and consolidated center of anxiety about the credit of the city and the dangers of heavy burdens upon real estate.

Disturbing reports of the size and management of the city debts were circulated during the campaign of 1870. Just prior to the election Tweed called in six leading citizens including John Jacob Astor and allowed them to glance at the financial ledgers. After hasty inspection, the six issued a reassuring statement: provision had been made for payment of the debt and the city's accounts were properly kept.[8]

Rumors of the size of the debt grew more persistent in the spring of 1871. In April, the Berlin *Zeitschrift fur Kapital und Rente* noted that only the reputation of the underwriters, Rothschild and the Discounts Gesellschaft, encouraged it to trust the soundness of the New York securities listed on the Berlin exchange.[9] Dexter Hawkins—lawyer, advocate of public education, friend of "nonsectarian" charities and bitter foe of the Catholic

---

[5] Linton Wells, "The House of Seligman," (typescript in the New York Historical Society, 1931), I, p. 156.
[6] *New York Herald,* October 27, 1871.
[7] *New York Herald,* November 9, 1871; *New York Times,* November 3, 1871.
[8] *New York Times,* November 1 and 7, 1870.
[9] Zeitschrift fur Kapital und Rente, VII (Supplement, 1872).

Church—argued in June that city expenses in 1869 and 1870 had far exceeded the budget. He charged that temporary revenue bonds issued in anticipation of taxes had been funded into long-term securities.[10] Comptroller Connolly, who had not issued a report for two years, and Mayor Hall attempted to reassure investors that all was well. Hall protested that the cry for economy was an old cry but the need of the moment was "planning for posterity." [11]

In July the rumors of excessive borrowing were confirmed. The story is a familiar one.[12] In the winter of 1870 James Watson, the county auditor, was thrown from his sleigh and fatally injured. Negligence, for which thieves pay highly, allowed a political friend of James O'Brien to be appointed in Watson's place. O'Brien was a local politician and former sheriff who had been denied a large claim he maintained against the city. He had led an unsuccessful factional fight against Tweed in 1870. With a friend as auditor, the discontented ex-sheriff soon had in his hands a careful copy of secret city and county accounts.

One newspaper refused O'Brien's "scoop" and he offered it to Tweed's bitter enemy, the *Times*. On July 8, 1871 the paper published a long report of frauds in the rental of city armories. On July 22, whole pages were reproduced from the comptroller's books, indicating extravagances which dwarfed the armory payments. In the next several days revelations continued until, on July 29, the *Times* published 200,000 copies of a four-page supplement summarizing all the evidence at its disposal. One hundred seventy-five thousand dollars had been spent on carpets for the new county court house, $7,500 for thermometers and $400,000 for safes. The special Board of Audit had "accepted" bills with a vengeance.

Bankers immediately refused to extend any further credit to the city. It is impossible to say how much the financiers knew of the corruption before the *Times'* disclosures. The bankers

---

[10] *New York Times*, June 20, 1871.
[11] *Irish American*, June 24, 1871; *New York Times*, June 13, 1871.
[12] Tweed has attracted many journalistic writers. See, for example, Denis Tilden Lynch, *"Boss" Tweed, The Story of a Grim Generation* (New York: Blue Ribbon Books, 1927); and William A. Bales, *Tiger in the Streets* (New York: Dodd, Mead, 1962).

could no longer endorse city securities once the first accounts had been published. They had no assurance that funds would be used for the capital improvements for which they were intended. The city was unable to sell even its short-term revenue bonds. Tax collections were slowed as businessmen refrained from taking advantage of the discount which rewarded early payment. The Berlin Stock Exchange refused to allow New York bonds to appear on its official lists. The *Commercial and Financial Chronicle* commented anxiously in August on the concentration of speculative municipal securities and mortgages in the hands of savings banks. A panic in the operations of the savings institutions, the *Chronicle* warned, would have wide repercussions.[13]

The decision to refuse credit to the city made it imperative to break the Ring even before the November 7 election. An interest payment of $2,700,000 on city bonds was due on November 1. Between November 1 and January 1 about $25,000,000 of short term acceptances were to be returned for payment. Failure of the city to meet its obligations would have impaired the value of bonds already issued. Henry Clews, a leading private banker and broker, argued that every New York banking house would suffer from the collapse of the city's credit.[14]

Tweed, repeating the successful tactics of 1870, offered the Chamber of Commerce an opportunity to look at the city's books. The Chamber refused. A committee of bankers and merchants was finally formed but, to Tweed's dismay, it reported in October that all confidence had been lost. "The demands upon the city treasury," it concluded, "will necessitate the borrowing of large sums of money at an early date. . . . Your committee regards as futile any attempts to borrow these large sums while the city is controlled by its present management."[15]

Tweed's opponents had to move quickly if the November 1 deadline was to be met. A great reform meeting at Cooper Union

[13] *Journal of Commerce*, August 31, 1871; *Commercial and Financial Chronicle*, XII (August 5, 1871), p. 166.

[14] Joint Investigating Committee of Supervisors, Aldermen and Associated Citizens, *Proceedings to Examine the Public Accounts of the City and County of New York* (New York, 1872), pp. 124–126; *New York Herald*, September 19, 1871.

[15] *New York Times*, October 28, 1871.

on September 4, 1871, resolved that the "wisest and best citizens" should run the city government. Bond issues should be public, and legal provision should be made to prevent unauthorized issues. If necessary, city officers should be elected "in such a manner as to secure the representation of the . . . minority as well as the majority." [16]

The meeting appointed an executive Committee of Seventy, chaired by Henry Stebbins, banker and former president of the Central Park Commission, to guide the attack on the Ring. The committee included figures who were merely prestigious together with those who merged prestige with power, a sampling of anti-Tammany Democrats, influential members of the German community, leading lawyers, businessmen with records of municipal reform activity and a few political celebrities such as John A. Dix and William Evarts. The list included at least eighteen bankers and brokers whose names appeared over and over again during the decade as advisers to city officials. In this group were B. B. Sherman, president of the Merchants National Bank; John A. Stewart, organizer of the United States Trust Company, the largest fiduciary institution in the city; William R. Vermilye, private banker and trustee of the Mutual Life Insurance Company; and Samuel D. Babcock, president of the United States Mortgage Company.

Tweed's political enemies flocked to the reform cause. Democratic leaders principally interested in national politics and discontented local party workers, Republicans and Germans, volunteered their aid. The high-level Democratic attack was led by Samuel Tilden, as head of the state Democratic committee, and August Belmont, national party chairman. After a long and uneasy alliance they broke with Tweed. "I fear," Tilden confided to a friend, "that the impression will spread throughout the country that "the evils and abuses in the local government of the city of New York are general characteristics of the Democratic Party and would occur in the Federal government if that party should come into power in Washington." [17]

---

[16] *New York Times*, September 5, 1871, supplement.
[17] John Bigelow, ed., *Letters and Literary Memorials of Samuel J. Tilden* (New York: Harper, 1908), I, p. 273.

Tweed had not been sparing in his patronage. Judicious arrangements had given him considerable influence in the city Republican organization, but he had begun to lose his grip on the opposition even before the *Times'* attack. Tammany subversion was a rhetorical issue in the intra-party fight between the two Republican United States Senators, Roscoe Conkling and Reuben Fenton. Conkling's victory in 1871 led to the reorganization of the Republican General Committee, the ruling party organ in the city, loosening Tweed's hold. As the Boss slipped, the Republicans were ready to jump on him.[18]

German Democrats who felt they had been denied their due by Tammany's leaders, rejoiced at Tweed's predicament. The Irish had moved into positions of leadership in the Democratic Party in the sixties, and they were not overly disposed to share the spoils. The separate German Democratic General Committee protested the Irish cast of the party in 1870 and was ready in the following year to support reform.[19] Oswald Ottendorfer, editor of the largest German language newspaper in the city, the *New Yorker Staats-Zeitung,* was in the front ranks of the reform battle.

Tweed's success in centralizing authority bred discontent among local party workers. Rebellious local leaders complained in 1870 that Tweed and Sweeny worked only for themselves and left the real workers and reliable adherents of the party, "out in the cold." The *Times,* in March, 1871, published an interview with an unidentified local politician. Tweed, Sweeny and Connolly had risen so far above the level of the local boys, he reported, that rebellion was swelling from below.[20]

There was some diffidence about a "low" political alliance in reform ranks but William F. Havemeyer, former mayor and a leader of the Committee of Seventy had, at least at this point, a firm grasp of reality. Respectable men, Havemeyer complained

---

[18] DeAlva Stanwood Alexander, *A Political History of the State of New York* (New York: Henry Holt, 1909), III, pp. 261–262; *New York Times,* October 7, 1870, August 12 and 24, 1871.
[19] *New York Times,* April 26, 1870, November 8, 1871; Matthew Breen, *Thirty Years of City Politics* (New York, 1899), pp. 274–275.
[20] *New York Times,* April 23, 1870, March 10, 1871.

to Tilden, were only a nuisance in politics. O'Brien was worth forty of them.[21]

Events moved rapidly after the September 4 meeting. Judge George Barnard, hitherto Tweed's loyal judicial ally, issued a temporary injunction on September 7 restraining the Comptroller or any other official from issuing additional bonds or making any expenditures. Barnard ordered funds put aside to meet the forthcoming interest payments. The injunction precipitated a crisis. Crowds of workingmen gathered around City Hall clamoring for their pay as the November 1 deadline drew nearer. Would Tweed be bold enough to use the threat of riot against the financiers, or was he too involved himself to risk the city's defaulting on its debt? The possibility of violence emerged from the promise of order.

There was panic in the municipal government. The comptroller's office was ransacked on September 11 and his records stolen. Tweed, Sweeny and Hall pressed Connolly to resign, hoping that a sacrificial lamb would satisfy their critics. Connolly was understandably bitter, and Havemeyer and Tilden were able to convince him to remain in office, denying Hall the opportunity of nominating a successor. Connolly agreed to appoint a deputy comptroller to assume actual direction of the city's financial affairs.[22]

Andrew H. Green was sworn in as deputy comptroller over Hall's vociferous protests on September 18. He faced two immediate tasks. With a cash balance in the treasury of $2,500,000 he had to meet the interest payment due November 1 and satisfy the claims of unpaid workers. Judge Barnard's original injunction was modified to allow for the payment of the workers but new loans were still interdicted. Green proceeded to borrow for the city in his own name. The Clearing House, advanced $500,000. Several individual banks undertook to pay specific groups of

---

[21] William F. Havenmeyer to Tilden, New York, October 25, 1871, in John Bigelow, ed., *Letters and Literary Memorials of Samuel J. Tilden* (New York: Harper, 1908).
[22] Andrew H. Green, *A Year's Record of a Reformer* (New York, 1872), pp. 8–12.

employees.[23] Barnard, on October 2, modified his injunction to allow the city to borrow up to $5,000,000 in order to maintain its credit. He specifically prohibited any borrowing by the departments still under Tweed's control.

At the beginning of October, the newspapers for the first time reported the loan which Belmont had negotiated for the Rothschilds. The loan was an obvious example of the funding of revenue bonds into long-term securities. The city had been cheated, the *Evening Post* stormed. The transaction had not been entirely completed and should not be. Green and Stebbins did not agree. They announced that they were satisfied that the contract was the best that could have been made. Belmont was anxious for further security and asked Tilden to convince Green to sign the bonds personally. He was unwilling to affront the European market with Connolly's signature.[24]

The Tweed Ring was virtually dead by the middle of October. Only the final blows had to be delivered. Tilden was the most important of the executioners. The *Times'* revelations, showing that obviously fraudulent bills had been accepted, demonstrated Tweed's guilt only indirectly. Tilden filed an affidavit on October 25 directly tracing money from city contractors to Tweed's bank account. The very next day Tweed was arrested. Governor Hoffman volunteered the complete legal resources of the state and appointed a special prosecutor, Charles O'Conor, dean of the New York bar.

The reformers utilized their financial power with great skill. With somewhat less acumen, they were able to hold together a political coalition through the election. Old-line Democrats swung into line as did a large group of young Democratic lawyers. They could not be dissuaded by the plea that was heard at Tweed's rallies: "One no more goes outside the party to purify it than one goes outside the Church." [25]

[23] *Ibid.*

[24] Wheeler H. Peckham to Tilden, New York, October 16, 1871, in John Bigelow, ed., *Letters and Literary Memorials of Samuel J. Tilden* (New York: Harper, 1908).

[25] Mark D. Hirsch, *William C .Whitney, Modern Warwick* (New York: Dodd, Mead, 1948), p. 61; John Bigelow, ed., *Letters and Literary Memorials of Samuel J. Tilden,* (New York: Harper, 1908), I, p. 289; *Irish-American,* September 30, 1871.

On November 2, Henry G. Stebbins delivered the final report of the Committee of Seventy. "There is not in the history of villainy," he declared, "a parallel for the gigantic crime against property conspired by the Tammany Ring." He detailed the manner and the danger of the Ring's finances. "If we fail to punish them," he concluded, "will not the capitalists and merchants of Europe logically conclude that our institutions are a failure, that the strength of American credit is gone and that it is unsafe to lend to and sell to a people whose rulers are thieves and whose legislators are robbers and rascals?" [26]

Exchanges and stores all over the city were closed on election day, 1871. When the ballots were counted Tweed had been re-elected as a state senator but his associates on every side had been defeated. The four other Tammany senators lost their seats by margins as high as five to one. Only a handful of Tammany assemblymen and aldermen were returned. The reform ticket did particularly well in German and native-born districts, but its city-wide margin of close to two-to-one suggests that it had gained support in every class and group.

Charges of widespread voting fraud, particularly in Tweed's home district, make it difficult to trust the final figures or to define clearly the real allegiance of the voters. The same difficulty plagued politicians. They enjoyed no pre-election polls, no scientific voting studies, to inform them of the voters' preferences. Frequently, to reduce their uncertainty, they resorted clumsily to stuffing boxes and buying votes. "The ballots made no result," Tweed quite frankly admitted later, "the counters made the result." [27] Sadly, the politicians were probably more corrupt than they had to be. In the absence of adequate information, it was better to overestimate an opponent's strength than to be caught short when the ballots were counted.

The first battle had been won. A major crisis had been averted and the bankers were relieved. Two of the savings banks

---

[26] *New York Times*, November 3, 1871.

[27] Tweed described his political methods to a committee of investigating aldermen in 1877. Board of Aldermen, *Report of a Special Committee of the Board of Aldermen Appointed to Investigate the Ring Frauds, Together with the Testimony Elicited During Their Investigation* (New York, 1878), pp. 133–137.

closely associated with the Ring failed but there was no general collapse.

The legacy of the Tweed Ring remained. Some of Tweed's friends left the city never to return. Others, including the Boss himself, began a long series of court battles. For almost a decade, until his death in 1878, the heaving figure of the master political entrepreneur loomed over Manhattan. He had held the city together—in his fashion. Could the city be coordinated in any other way or was it too much "Boss Tweed's New York"? Could honest men act as effectively as thieves?

Measuring the dimensions of Tweed's thievery taxed every accounting skill in the city. The pattern adopted by the Ring slowly became clear. They had allowed contractors to overcharge the city and then had received a kick-back on the lavish profits. It was almost impossible to define how much had actually been stolen. Estimates varied from forty to one hundred million dollars. In the wake of the Ring's fall, Andrew Green, as the new Comptroller, struggled to find out what obligations had been contracted and when they would fall due. Like a driver dragged in two directions by a team of wild horses his first impulse was desperately to pull in the reins.

NINE

In Pursuit of Economy

Green wanted to stop the world so that the accountants could check the ledgers. This was clearly impossible because the fall of the Ring had reopened political debate in the city to a host of contesting claims, values, and hopes. Tweed had resolved this debate by paying rival interests in their own coin—social welfare in one pocket, roads in another, cash in still a third (including his own). The "big pay-off" was discredited by the revelations of its enormous costs. Developing a public consensus without paying for it was difficult since the images men brought into political debate were almost always limited and local. The city required rapid transportation—but "not on my street at my expense." The waterfront was decrepit—but established shippers should not be disturbed. New York was raw and open—but "my neighborhood is finished."

Honest administrators and party leaders, contending with the massive complexities of a great metropolis, faced an even more difficult task of coordination than their corrupt predecessors. Replacing the big pay-off required massive investments in a communications network and in the techniques for dealing with complex data. While these investments were debated, the ship of state rocked precariously. Plans were frequently changed and appropriations delayed. As a result, the development program moved erratically. The population flowed into areas which had not been drained in advance, where the unpaved streets alternated between mud and dust and the houses were chronically short of water. Relations between social groups were strained by an attack upon the legitimacy of democratic politics. The new party leaders who replaced Tweed were trained to respect the localism of the city, even as they were accused of creating an absolute dictatorship.

Economic theory suggests that businessmen will invest in the enterprise where they anticipate the marginal returns on their capital will be the greatest. Debates over expenditures for information in the last decades of the nineteenth century often generated more heat than light because it was almost impossible to specify either the marginal returns or the beneficiaries of a potential investment. This difficulty is clear if we examine an exception to the general rule. One of the great issues of the seventies was the reform of administrative procedures on the Erie Canal through which a great deal of American wheat passed on its way to international markets. On the competitive Liverpool exchange, the president of the New York Produce Exchange explained, the difference in cost of a single penny "may determine the question whether millions of bushels shall be supplied by this country, or shall be drawn from the ample fields of Hungary or Southern Russia." [1] The product, grain, was homogeneous and the impact of small changes in costs and prices was decisive.

Usually the benefits of public investments were harder to measure. A group of physicians in the middle sixties had demonstrated that the city paid heavily for the failure to invest in public health and housing regulation.[2] How great were the costs? Who paid them? If other cities were similarly burdened, was New York pressed to improve immediately? What were the marginal benefits of each additional expenditure for information and control? Was it possible that at certain levels of expenditure, the costs outweighed the benefits?

The stark difficulties of answering these questions without a large initial investment in accounting procedures and information services polarized debate around two harsh alternatives: cut costs and leave the world alone or spend, spend, spend. In the wake of

[1] Franklin Edson, *Letters on the Reduction of Canal Tolls, April 7, 1875* (New York, 1875).
[2] Council of Hygiene and Public Health of the Citizens Association of New York, *Report Upon the Sanitary Condition of the City* (New York, 1865).

the Tweed Ring, New York was engaged in a headlong pursuit of economy.

Andrew H. Green, as comptroller, played a central role in the process by which public development of the city was curtailed. Green had always argued for orderly advance. He continued to urge the "progress of the great public improvements for the development or adornment of the city." At the same time, Green was committed to a series of proposals to limit expenditures, lower the tax rate, and prevent the expansion of the debt "except for great and unusual emergencies." These proposals, as Mayor Hall argued, could not help but restrict municipal development.[3]

Green was allied with "reform" groups whose principal concern was the expansion of minority power in city politics in order to cut the public budget. A new city charter to meet this end was passed by the Republican legislature—only to be vetoed by the Democratic governor. The legislative vote hewed closely to party lines. The only Republican to oppose the charter in the assembly was elected from the Twenty-first Assembly District in the northernmost portion of the city.[4]

The viewpoint of many of the reformers who leaped to Green's side in 1872 was explained at a rally in September. J. M. Van Cott of the Council of Political Reform complained that $50,000,000 or even $25,000,000 (which was closer to the actual levy), was a heavy tax burden for a city that was essentially developed. Is it conceivable, he argued, that "fifty million dollars, or the half of it, is a fair sum for liquidating the current expenses of the administration of a city lying within so small a geographical area," with its streets already laid out, its parks "almost completed," its "system of sewerage already established?"[5]

Van Cott's view of the city was most strongly expressed in the long debate over the widening of Broadway, a debate only closed by court decision at the very end of 1872. Property owners

[3] *New York Tribune*, June 14, 29; July 11, 16, 1872; Green to Mayor Havemeyer, January 18, 1878, Mayors Papers, Letter Book, February, 1868-May, 1873.

[4] The proposed charter is described in the *New York Tribune*, January 20, 1872.

[5] *New York Tribune*, September 24, 1872.

in the lower city argued that improvement of the avenue, far from benefiting them, would bring the new areas into competition with their settled region. They were able, as beneficiaries of decentralization, to delay action for four years.[6]

Though the battle of Broadway was lost, the victory over the Tweed Ring reinforced the assertion that the city was "finished." Any further improvements should be made and paid for by those uniquely benefited by "progress." In the spring of 1872 the legislature prevented the city from assessing property owners without their consent for repavement of the streets adjoining their plots. Green successfully sponsored a bill providing that assessments could not be vacated for technical reasons unless substantial inequity resulted from the irregularities. No longer, he hoped, would the city informally subsidize the construction of new streets.[7]

During the debate on the charter early in 1872, work in the city departments crept to a standstill in expectation of imminent reorganization. During the ensuing months Green used every effort to restrict expenditures to those absolutely required by law. He carefully audited all bills. Every claim was subject to long and thorough examination while laborers and contractors were left unpaid. They waited, clamoring for their money. Court dockets overflowed with suits to force payment.[8]

Green's auditing procedures made him a hated man. "We have kept our men at work without pay just as long as we can," the superintendent of the street cleaning bureau protested in May, 1872. "Their grocers refuse to trust them any longer, and, in some instances, their landlords have turned them into the street. They regard you [Green] as the sole cause of their sufferings, and their feelings in regard to you are of a desperate character—so desperate, in fact, that dangerous results may follow." [9]

This threat of violence was not to be taken lightly. Many of the political disputes of the seventies are easily passed over as

[6] *New York Tribune*, December 25, 1872.
[7] *Laws, 1872*, c. 580; *New York Tribune*, May 25, 27, 1872.
[8] See Green's explanation of his procedures and problems, Circular No. 7, March 3, 1873, Mayors Papers, Box 41.
[9] *New York Tribune*, May 25, 1872.

trivial debates over administrative procedures and forms. These debates, trivial as they may seem, were at the very center of the business of running the city. The lines of communication and the distribution of authority within the government were problematical. Decisions on substantive issues, therefore, were burdened by insistent procedural questions of "how things were to be done." At times, procedural issues totally obscured substantive problems. Green, attempting to work out a series of standard administrative rules, seemed to have a special knack for arguing over the order of signing a document. A breakdown in the day-to-day operations of governmental agencies led to conflict and violence. City laborers rioted because their pay had been lost in an administrative tangle.[10]

The most outspoken critic of Green's course was George Van Nort, the superintendent of public works. Van Nort had been employed by the Parks Department under Sweeny. A Republican, he was appointed to replace Tweed in the Department of Public Works as part of the bipartisan bargain which had destroyed the Ring. With enormous patronage at his disposal, he immediately became a figure of importance within his party. He was able in 1872 to persuade the legislature to transfer to him the remaining authority of the Parks Department over uptown streets and to gain new appropriations for paving.[11]

The dangerous condition of the streets, Van Nort complained in April, was Green's responsibility. The suspension of payments had forced the cessation of both new work and repairs. The refusal of the comptroller to pay contractors, he argued, resulted in a large number of men being thrown out of their jobs "at a season when they were most in need of their daily earnings, and interrupting the prosecution of necessary improvements." He had, in addition, been unable to begin work on many of the projects authorized by the Common Council in 1871 because the ordinances had not been properly advertised according to law. The appropriations he was able to drag out of the legislature over Green's opposition, he contended, were totally inadequate and

[10] See the extensive correspondence between Green and Wickham over the signing of warrants, Mayors Papers, Letterbook, January, 1875-May, 1876.
[11] *Real Estate Record and Builder's Guide*, IX (June 8, 1872), p. 263.

did not allow him to improve the streets in the tenement districts where owners refused to be voluntarily taxed for resurfacing.[12]

The degree to which the city was finished was seriously debated in the election campaign of 1872, though it is impossible to discern the impact of the issue upon the electorate through the fog of tangled political alliances. Democrats and Liberal Republicans supported Horace Greeley in the race for the presidency. Republicans chose John Dix, a former Democrat, to run for governor. James O'Brien's supporters claimed credit for the local reform victory in 1871 and demanded recognition as the regular city Democratic organization.

Tammany Hall itself was the site of intense conflict. Several ward leaders attempted to seize power in the wake of Tweed's collapse. They were outmaneuvered by a group of nationally oriented business and political leaders who had, through the Tweed years, retained a hand in the Tammany Society. The society was a "social" organization of the party elite and owned the building in which the Democratic Republican General Committee of the City of New York (Tammany Hall) met. Control of the keys to the building was turned into control of the party.[13]

The new leaders included Tilden, Abram Hewitt, Augustus Schell and Horace Clark. Schell and Clark were old party figures and directors of the New York Central Railroad. Hewitt was a New Jersey iron maker who had first become engaged by politics after the war. The old club, he insisted, "is still dear to the hearts of honest Democrats in this city and elsewhere. The work of reform can be more readily and effectively carried on by availing of its organization, its traditions and its machinery, than by any new invention of political doctrinaires." [14]

The head of the new "reformed" Tammany was John Kelly, the first Irish leader of the Democratic Party. For ten years, from 1858 to 1868, Kelly was County Sheriff but after quarreling with Tweed he left the city for a prolonged stay in Europe. The new

[12] Department of Public Works of the City of New York, *Second Annual Report, For the Year Ending April 10, 1872* (New York, 1872), pp. 10, 22–23.
[13] Matthew P. Breen, *Thirty Years of New York Politics, Up-to-Date* (New York, 1899); pp. 376–383.
[14] *New York Tribune,* October 8, 1872.

party leader was a man of great pride who made deserved claims to culture and respectability. He lived in the fashionable Murray Hill district and in 1876 married the niece of John McCloskey, the first American Cardinal. In Kelly, the Irish middle class asserted its claim to a place at the dais. The new leader was far removed from both the working class and the low wardheelers with whom his critics tended to lump him. Nevertheless, when he was excited, Kelly's grammar failed and he proudly boasted that he had been educated in the "school of life." [15]

The party Kelly led was a model of diffused authority. Tweed had hardly interfered with this structural decentralization. Kelly, wrapping himself in the mantle of reform, attacked it directly. The Central Committee on Organization asked for sweeping powers to reorganize district associations by removing objectionable members and appointing new ones in their place. The local leaders demurred before such an extreme measure of centralization. They allowed the committee to remove delegates but insisted that the remaining district members jointly choose replacements. The central committee, led by Kelly, used its new authority to purge Tweed's allies. When it encountered resistance, Hewitt threatened to withdraw his "faction" unless Kelly was sustained. [16]

Kelly tried to bring all of the 1871 reformers into the Tammany fold. He suggested an alliance with the Committee of Seventy even at the cost of the resentment of many district leaders. They thought he was pandering to a clique whose sense of importance was out of all proportion to its real political influence. [17] The new "Boss" encountered the first of a series of rejections which were to shape the course of city politics and growth. The Seventy nominated Havemeyer for mayor and endorsed the entire Republican slate. The Tammany nomination went to Abraham Lawrence, a lawyer with a good Democratic family background.

[15] James F. McLaughlin, *The Life and Times of John Kelly, Tribune of the People* (New York, 1885), is a contemporary defense of Kelly. See the *New York Tribune*, October 8, 1872 and September 28, 1876, for samples of Kelly's style.

[16] Democratic Republican General Committee of the City of New York, *By-Laws for the Year 1872* (New York, 1872); *New York Tribune*, October 2, 1872.

[17] *New York Tribune*, October 10, 1872.

It is frequently said that the Irish conquered the American city but did not know what to do with the kingdom they had won. There is some truth in the statement. The Irish-American community of the late nineteenth century was undergoing a process of change in which individual achievement loomed larger than social unity. Getting ahead in politics, like success in business, was a sign of individual achievement and ethnic glory. It had very little to do with public policy. The Irish were still in the "free enterprise" stage of Americanization. Beyond this, the Irish came to power but could not command respect. Even "American" bosses in "American" cities had difficulty integrating the sprawling giants of the late nineteenth century. Scorned leaders could hope for even less success in shaping creative roles for city governments.[18]

Lawrence and O'Brien, nominated for mayor by his faction meeting in Apollo Hall, charged that Havemeyer was an old man (he was sixty-eight and had been mayor in 1848 and 1849) who was behind the times and basically opposed to the development program. A speaker at an open air Lawrence rally caught the spirit of their common indictment. Mr. Havemeyer, he sniffed, "was well enough when New York had 40,000 inhabitants, but he is not alive to the onward march of the city at the present day. His idea would be, if I might judge from his past record, that it did not make any difference whether a man had rapid transit to get to Harlem or whether he had to walk there." By 1872, the real possibility and desire to get to Harlem had grown so that it did make a difference. It was also critically important that New York had "the meanest set of piers and docks of any city in the world."[19]

Both Lawrence and O'Brien played repeatedly on the double

---

[18] Daniel Moynihan, "When the Irish Ran New York," *Reporter*, XXIV (June 8, 1961), pp. 32–34, links the Irish organization of the city and Irish attitudes towards social change to the legacies of the home isle and Catholicism. This paragraph suggests that there is an intermediate step between traditional conservatism and reform. This step—insistent individualism—is a product of Americanization. It is subtly intertwined with the forms of traditionalism and appears to have some of the same implications. Dorothy Ross, "The Irish-Catholic Immigrants, 1880–1900: A Study in Social Mobility," (unpublished masters essay, Columbia University, 1959), pp. 78–109, demonstrates the growth of a concept of secular piety in the Irish community.

[19] *New York Tribune*, November 4, 1872.

theme of the necessity of new projects for the welfare of the city
and for the promise they offered of employment. Public improvements of interest to the upper wards, Lawrence insisted, should
not be stopped but should be carried on with dispatch "not only
because it is necessary for the health and enjoyment of our people, but because these improvements gave employment to a large
class of our population." They should be carried on as economi-
cally as possible but their "spirit and scope should not be circumscribed." He promised, in the best American tradition, that he
would be the real mayor and would not be bossed.[20]

A group of real estate brokers addressed a letter to the candidates. Did they favor, the brokers asked, a "speedy and vigorous
prosecution of the public works now in hand to completion?"
Would they, furthermore, favor a "liberal system of public improvements in the future, with such changes in the administration of that system as shall secure unity of counsel and action?"
Finally, the brokers asked, did the candidates favor a system of
rapid transit, "which shall provide the largest accommodation to
our citizens at the lowest cost, and to this end that it be done by
the city as a municipal work?" All three candidates hedged on
the issues of municipal construction of a rapid transit system but
only Havemeyer seemed to entertain doubts about the absolute
need for such a system. They all affirmed their interest in public
improvements though Havemeyer's statement was particularly
insistent on efficiency and economy.[21]

Havemeyer's letter to a German-American reform group in
October suggested his essential view of the city. New York, he
wrote, was the center of an empire which reached across continents and oceans. The special role of the city government was to
safeguard New York's external contacts. Commerce, for example,
should not be "crippled by the unjust and unnecessary exactions
of official tyranny." The internal web of relationships did not
engage Havemeyer's imagination. He was more intimately aware
of the connections between New York and the outside world than
he was of the connections between groups and areas within the
city. (A connection with Brooklyn was a rather special problem.
Havemeyer denounced Roebling's grand scheme as a project

[20] *New York Tribune,* November 4, 1872.
[21] *New York Tribune,* November 4, 1872.

At the center of the telegraph network, circa 1870. The rites of passage limited the imagination. *Bettmann Archive*

"conceived in sin, born in iniquity and which, like all similar creations, must end in disaster for all concerned in it." It would be of absolutely no use to New York.) Internally, it was simply necessary for the city government to ensure that "accessions of population and capital" should not be retarded by "excessive and onerous taxation." He was a partisan of decentralization.[22]

The Democratic vote on election day was small and divided. Havemeyer carried normal Republican areas and was elected.

It is tempting to think that the new mayor's critics were correct, that he was simply an old man, grown cantankerous with age, inflexible in his choice of means, and rigidly insistent on his own rectitude. The criticism assumes that a younger man would have been more flexible as a "reform" administrator and obscures the essential continuity between Havemeyer's early and late career. He was of the generation of upright Jacksonians, better described as aristocratic than as enemies of privilege. They boasted of their ability to resist popular passions rather than of their responsiveness to public opinion. Havemeyer had inherited the beginnings of his sugar refining firm and had been president of the Bank of North America and the New York Savings Bank. His administration in the forties was marked by a stern insistence on economy. He nurtured the infant professional police force as an instrument to control endemic urban violence.[23]

Havemeyer in 1873 was committed to a double task. He wanted to cut taxes and to limit the growth of the debt. Many public projects of only local interest, he told the Common Council on January 6, found their way onto the general shoulders. The expansion of the debt must end. Development must again be paid for by the local beneficiaries.[24]

[22] New York Tribune, October 19, 1872. For Havemeyer's indictment of the bridge see New York Tribune, April 13, 1874.
[23] James Grant Wilson and John Fiske, eds., Appleton's Cycleopaedia of American Biography (New York, 1900), III, pp. 116–117. The concept of Havemeyer as an old Jacksonian is suggested by the argument of Lee Benson, The Concept of Jacksonian Democracy, New York as a Test Case (Princeton: Princeton University Press, 1961), particularly pp. 64–68.
[24] William F. Havemeyer, Inaugural Message of Hon. William F. Havemeyer, Mayor of the City of New York, January 6th, 1873 (New York, 1873), pp. 5–6.

The new mayor found in the two years of his administration that his two objectives were not entirely compatible. The mayor and comptroller fought a running battle with Superintendent of Public Works Van Nort and with the association of West Side real estate owners, but the commitments authorized by law could not be entirely denied. During 1873 and 1874 a great deal of new land was purchased by the city, Central Park was improved, Broadway, Seventh, and Tenth Avenues were widened and several new piers were constructed. The accomplishments, compared with the promises of the development program, seemed rather meagre. Tweed, for all his faults, the *Tribune* sighed on August 7, 1873, would have "stolen the city rich." [25]

The financial frustration of Havemeyer's administration was apparent in the debt and tax figures. The tax rate in 1872 was $2.90 on every $100 of assessed property. It dropped to $2.50 in 1873 but rose again to $2.80 in 1874 and to $2.94 in 1875. The debt, which was approximately $88,000,000 at the end of 1871, stood at $115,000,000 at the close of 1874.[26]

Havemeyer was pleased that the burden of taxes was, at least in his eyes, more fairly distributed than it had been under Tweed. Until May, 1873, the Department of Taxes and Assessments, which fixed property valuations, included several "legacies" of the Tweed era. Property in the Twelfth, Nineteenth, and Twenty-second Wards, covering all of Manhattan Island above 40th Street, was valued at roughly $216,000,000 in 1872. Assessments rose in 1873, after the change in personnel, to $236,000,000. The assessors made only minor adjustments in their estimates for the rest of the city.

[25] Uptown improvements are conveniently tabulated in William R. Martin, *A Communication Relative to the Prosecution of Public Improvements in This City* (New York, 1875), pp. 21–35. New pavements are listed in the Department of Public Works, *Report for the Quarter Ending December 31, 1877* (New York, 1878), p. 12. The work of the Dock Department during the entire decade is summarized in Commissioners of Accounts, *Report of an Examination into the Affairs of the Department of Docks from May, 1870 to April 30, 1881* (New York, 1881).
[26] Edward Dana Durand, *The Finances of New York City* (New York: Macmillan, 1898), p. 375.

The Commissioners of Taxes and Assessments in August, 1873 vigorously defended their policy. Uptown owners, they reported, had pleaded for years that the market prices of their property reflected only a temporary speculative boom and that builders in new regions should be treated as "pioneers" and "benefactors" of the entire city. These pleas had been heeded in 1871 and 1872 but could no longer be sustained. Downtown owners, the commissioners argued, complained with a good deal of justice that they carried the burden of the northern city. The improvement of Fourth Avenue, for example, was solely for the benefit of uptown residents who were annoyed by the surface tracks, and yet was financed by general taxation.[27]

The attempt to economize crippled downtown development and had a curiously disjointed effect on the upper West Side. The city had rushed headlong into what was, perhaps, an extravagant program. The reform movement limited, but did not reorder, the pattern of development. Avenues were cut through the "wilderness," but the orderly preparation of areas with streets, sewers, water mains, parks, and schools was not attempted. West Side owners understandably complained that they did not receive the benefits for which they were assessed; that the East Side, relatively unblessed with improvements, prospered.[28]

Havemeyer's premonitions of imminent disaster seemed to be confirmed by the financial panic of September, 1873. During 1874, as the city momentarily found it more difficult to sell long-term securities, Green and Havemeyer became more insistent on limitations on all expenditures. The principal danger to the welfare of the city, the Mayor contended, was the great body of laws enacted under Tweed which authorized extensive public improvements. Every citizen, he argued, must be interested in the repeal

[27] Commissioners of Taxes and Assessments, *Taxes and Assessments in the City of New York, Report of the Commissioners, 1873* (New York, 1873), pp. 18–20.
[28] "Report of Hon. Wm. R. Martin, President, Upon the Subject of Laying-out the Twenty-third and Twenty-fourth Wards," in Board of Commissioners of the Department of Public Parks, *Minutes of the Proceedings for the Year Ending April 30, 1877* (New York, 1877), Document 73, pp. 22–23.

of the authority to push ahead with new public projects because "it involves millions of dollars, which are either to be collected by assessments, or to be thrown as a tax on the city, for making drives, boulevards, etc. far up on the Island and chiefly for private benefit." He denied the need for new reservoirs to protect the growing city's supply of water and recommended simply the expansion of aqueduct facilities. The city had already invested $1,500,000 in the Brooklyn Bridge and, he insisted, should refuse any further assistance. Public recreational facilities should not be designed on the grand and expensive scale which had been chosen for Central Park.[29] (Could Havemeyer have been the subject of Olmsted's story?)

Green associated himself with Havemeyer's position and rhetoric. Henry Stebbins, once again a member of the Park Commission, pressed for an expanded program uptown. The comptroller accused him of "obstructionism."

The time had come to look after the lower city, Green proclaimed. Rather than press uptown works a generation too early it would be better to improve downtown streets. No work at all should be done uptown until property owners showed a greater willingness to pay their assessments. "It is not just," he insisted, "that the property owners in the lower part of the city should be taxed to pay for uptown improvements which are solely for the benefit of the owners of these lots." Better spend the public money on the docks.[30]

Promoters in the new areas and the lower class were both forced to bear the burden of economy and were pressed in subsequent years into a curious political alliance. In March, 1874 Havemeyer reassured a committee of the Harvard Association that "destitution and suffering" has been "promptly and adequately met by private donations and the various Christian and charitable institutions" and has not "been as general as to warrant the interference of the Municipal authorities."[31] Public outdoor relief

---

[29] Mayor of the City of New York, *Message to the Common Council, January 19, 1874* (New York, 1874), pp. 84–85, 18–20, 28–29.
[30] *New York Tribune*, July 14, 1874.
[31] Havemeyer to Committee of the Harvard Association, March 7, 1874, Mayors Papers, Letter Book, March, 1873-January, 1875.

was discontinued in July and was only resumed on a severely limited scale in January, 1875—a thin soup for the destitute.

Real estate promoters encountered a similar skepticism in their appeals for aid. In February, 1874, Green and Chamberlain George Lane argued that the city's contract with the Union Ferry Company, which exempted it from a franchise tax in return for a reduction of rush hour fares, was illegal. Taxpayers were asked, improperly they thought, to subsidize the users of the ferry. Green and Lane dismissed the contention that the lower fares benefited the city as a whole. Ferry boat owners, they insisted, had invested in real estate in Long Island and New Jersey. Cheap fares were to their own interest. The commissioners of the sinking fund, responsible for the franchise, began a long litigation to void the contract first negotiated by Tweed.[32]

Both the Dock Department's plans for the waterfront and the hopes of the city for a rapid transit line suffered from the demands for economy and the reinsistance on decentralization. The docks and transit lines were, however, affected in significantly different ways. Responsibility for the waterfront remained fixed in public hands while the problems of rapid transportation were shifted to private shoulders.

Only two sets of railroad tracks entered the city at the beginning of the seventies, those of the New York and Harlem on the East Side and those of the Hudson River Railroad on the West. Both roads were part of Cornelius Vanderbilt's railroad empire. The Commodore was anxious to prevent the construction of a rapid transit line which would allow other railroads to enter New York on its tracks or would compete for the commuter traffic carried by the New York and Harlem. The Commodore, a Bronx developer contended in 1879, had stood for twenty years "like a bull dog on the Harlem River declaring that no one should cross but by his permission."[33]

Vanderbilt, like Tweed, was a figure of legends. It is difficult to distinguish the boundaries of his influence, the precise character

[32] Mark D. Hirsch, *William C. Whitney, Modern Warwick* (New York; Dodd, Mead, 1948), pp. 100–101.
[33] Leonard Jerome to Mayor Edward Cooper, August 3, 1879, Mayors' Papers, Box 435.

of his purposes. He was at once bogeyman and real manipulator. One hot day in 1872 the aldermen were at each other's throats. "It is well known," Jenkins van Schaick, elected as a reformer, charged, "that Cornelius Vanderbilt understands how to fix committees of this board so that they do just what he wants them to do." His colleagues, up in arms. demanded a bill of particulars. "If you don't propose to expose such committees," one insisted, you have no business to make such remarks among gentlemen." Van Schaick cleverly avoided distinguishing between bogeyman and manipulator. "I don't make them among gentlemen," he quietly replied, concluding the matter.[34]

Vanderbilt's influence was not all covert. Some politicians didn't have to be bribed. An angry delegate to the Tammany judicial convention in October, 1872 stormed that the convention could not be "dictated to by the Central Railroad or Mr. Vanderbilt." Horace Clark, a director of the Central, sputtered in his chair on the podium.[35]

The Viaduct scheme had collapsed in Tweed's ruin so that at the beginning of 1873 the city remained without immediate hope for a rapid transit line along the entire length of Manhattan. The general discomfort was in the interests of Vanderbilt, the street railway and ferry companies, certain downtown property owners with long records of opposition to rapid transit, and the promoters of real estate on Long Island and New Jersey. Tweed had cut through the tangle of conflicting interests with his Viaduct Railroad. Havemeyer denounced both Vanderbilt and the street railway companies but was bent on economy. He had neither the corrupt motives nor the honest vision to act effectively.

Rapid transit lines were constructed in the second half of the decade by vigorous entrepreneurs using the instruments of government to meet their demands on their terms. The effort to have government mobilize capital failed.

The city did not similarly abandon its claims to leadership and control of the waterfront but the promise of the first days of the new Dock Department was almost immediately circumscribed. The first new acquisitions of land to fulfill McClellan's plan were made in the summer of 1872. The high cost of these initial purchases ensured that unless the city was willing to spend vast sums it would be a long time before the work was completed. Owners of waterfront property, including some of the wealthiest men in New York, fought the Dock Department tooth and nail. Extension of the bulkhead was prohibited in 1873 and the old commissioners were removed. They complained as they left office that Green had withheld funds appropriated for their use. The new commissioners adopted a mode of construction and a waterfront plan which was both cheaper and more circumscribed than McClellan had envisaged.[36]

The Havemeyer administration was committed to public improvement of the waterfront, if the cost was not too great. The mayor firmly rejected a proposal to turn harbor development over into private hands. A group of capitalists was able in 1874 to convince the legislature to authorize the New York Warehouse and Bulkhead Company to build a bulkhead, railroad, and roadway around the island and a series of steel piers. The new company, linked to the New York Central, would have installed Vanderbilt as a "bull dog" over the harbor.[37]

Merchant organizations called upon the governor to veto the bill. Havemeyer denounced the scheme as the "most gigantic monopoly of modern times." Governor Dix killed the bill in July with an angry veto. The city, he said, had lavished millions on the opening of streets in uptown areas in advance of public needs but had neglected the docks. The public must, however, remedy its own negligence. The attempt of the New York Warehouse and Bulkhead Company to control the waterfront was "monstrous." "It is a striking example of the grossest abuses of the day in legislation —the creation of great corporations, and the surrender of the rights of individuals and the interest of municipalities for their special benefit." "The crowning indignity of the bill," Dix declared, was the creation of the company as a "public corporation" equal in rank to the government of the city "which is despoiled and made tributary to it." The bill was deceptive. Under the guise of promoting only the public interest it freed the company from "the legal

[36] *New York Tribune*, October 5, 1872, April 26, 1873, March 9, 1874.
[37] *Commercial and Financial Chronicle*, XVI (May 17, 1873), pp. 648–649.

liabilities to which corporations created for private profit are subject." [38]

Dix was a better prophet than he knew of the political history of the rapid transit lines. There is, however, an element of irony in the prophesy. The transit lines, given into private hands, "despoiled" the city—but they were completed. The docks, which remained a public responsibility, were never rebuilt on a comprehensive plan. The reformers managed to create the conditions they decried. They were unable to develop any other consensus than an insistence on economy and decentralization.

[38] Charles Z. Lincoln, ed., *Messages of the Governors of New York State* (Albany: J. B. Lyon, 1909), VI, pp. 684–689.

TEN

Self-Confirming Suspicions:

The End of Reform

The attitudes which crippled the program of public improvements, destroyed the reform movement itself and imposed upon the city a formal governmental structure characterized by an intense suspicion of power.

In 1873 the legislature passed a new charter for New York which remained in force until 1897.[1] The charter was a compromise between the conflicting views of the Committee of Seventy and Republican politicians ("schemers and political adventurers," Havemeyer called them). Under the charter, a minority of the voters would enjoy increased representation in the unicameral Common Council. Three aldermen were to be selected annually from each of the city's five senate districts, but each voter could only vote for two candidates. An additional six aldermen were elected from the city at large, each voter choosing four.

The powers of the aldermen were carefully enumerated and severely limited. They were authorized, for example, to regulate the opening and cleaning of streets. In fact, responsibility for these and comparable tasks was retained in the legislature or delegated to administrative agencies. The Board of Aldermen, unable to raise taxes or contract debts, was basically a licensing agency. Under special circumstances it could delay or obstruct the execution of public policy but it could not initiate policy. Its most precious pre-

[1] *Laws, 1873,* c. 335.

rogative was the right to confirm the mayor's appointments. Impotent in almost every important area, the board was ineffective in even its small tasks. Mayor after mayor was forced to veto ordinances because they conflicted with the law, had already been passed or were based on patently false information.

Real power in the city was located in the separate departments and in three interdepartmental boards. The first of these three was the Board of the Commissioners of the Sinking Fund, composed of the mayor, recorder, chamberlain, comptroller, and the chairman of the Finance Committee of the Board of Aldermen. The board was entrusted with responsibility for the management of a portion—but not all—of the city debt. It controlled the sale or lease of all public property other than the wharves and piers.

The second of the three was the Board of Street Opening and Improvements, including the mayor, comptroller, commissioner of public works and the presidents of the Department of Parks and the Board of Aldermen. It was empowered to alter the street plan below 59th Street. It could, however, neither raise taxes nor contract debts.

Control over expenditures was given to the mayor, the comptroller, and the presidents of the Board of Aldermen and the Department of Taxes and Assessments sitting as a Board of Estimate and Apportionment. This board fixed the budget, was responsible for the issuance of most bonds and, for all intents and purposes, levied local taxes. Municipal salaries and the general direction of the course of development continued, however, to be defined by the legislature.

The mayor's real place in the system was uncertain. He was a member of each of the three interdepartmental boards. He could nominate and, with the approval of the governor, remove department heads. Nevertheless without a department of his own and with very indefinite rights of supervision, he often appeared outside the decision-making arena. The nastiest political conflicts of the seventies occurred when department heads contended that they had proprietary rights in their offices and could be removed only after "due process of law."

The comptroller enjoyed real authority. Every municipal expenditure required his signature. His rights of inquiry and his ability to delay payments gave him an important check on the processes of government. When Kelly replaced Green as comptroller in 1876 he combined, as had Tweed, both party and governmental leadership. If his opponents can be believed, it was precisely the extent of his potential influence and not his behavior which they opposed.

The attempt to exploit the potentialities of the one strong executive office in the city failed in the seventies. The division of administrative responsibility might have yielded substantial benefits comparable to those enjoyed by large decentralized corporations, if the division had been clear and the source of ultimate authority unchallenged. The city was, however, not a predecessor of General Motors. Debates over substantive policy were turned into arguments over the location of authority. It was generally expected that public offices would be used for partisan advantage because it was very difficult for New Yorkers to envisage genuine nonpartisanship. This endemic suspicion of motives tended to discourage the development of a neutral and responsible bureaucracy. The creation of bipartisan boards, as a protection against gross party manipulation, did not ensure effective government. Overlapping lines of executive, legislative, and judicial authority designed to check on public officials, made it difficult to depend on their performances. Green and Havemeyer repeatedly appealed to the courts against the legislature, or refused to execute a policy they opposed on the grounds that the initial authorization was unclear.[2]

Havemeyer was pleased with the new charter, though obtaining it cost him the support of the Republican Party organization. He soon lost the support of the Democrats as well. His first appointments to office, and most of his charter proposals, had been supported by Tammany Hall. This support vanished when Havemeyer attempted to replace the nine Democratic police justices with Republicans. The police justices were the lowest members of the judiciary but were close to the day-to-day affairs of ward politics. The justices tried petty thieves, gamblers, drunks, street walkers,

[2] The best example of this was Havemeyer's refusal to sign the warrants, allowing the city to pay its portion of the costs of covering Fourth Avenue. *New York Tribune*, June 8, 1874; Havemeyer to Corporation Council E. Delafield Smith, September 14, 1874, Mayors Papers, Letter Book, March, 1873-January, 1875.

and unlicensed liquor dealers. German Republicans were also angry with Havemeyer. They complained that they had not received their proper share of city patronage. The German and Irish immigrant aid societies complained that the new members of the Board of Emigration chosen by the mayor were neither "immigrants nor sons of immigrants." Uptown aldermen denounced increased valuations and limitations on public works. Havemeyer, by the fall of 1873, did not have the support of a single mass-based political organization. The Board of Aldermen left his appointments hanging fire.[3]

The comptroller was caught in a similar web of attacks. Officers of the ship-joiners and coopers union berated the city government for neglecting the working people. Wages on public works had been cut, employment diminished and "pauper labor permitted to do the work of citizens."[4] O'Brien denounced Green's policies as "unjust, impolitic and oppressive and eminently calculated to interfere with the prosperity and interests of our city." He had disregarded legal claims, opposed improvements essential to the "interests of capital and the employment of labor," and "impaired the efficiency of city offices."[5] The Board of Aldermen condemned the comptroller for evading and repudiating the payment of just claims against the city.[6] A group of lawyers fastened on the comptroller's treatment of claims. They revealed that the city, under Green and Havemeyer's direction, had paid two lobbyists in Albany to support bills for the funding of a sinking fund deficiency and to oppose public appropriations for repaving the streets and for limitation of the comptroller's authority to audit claims. The indictment of Green was bitter and complete. He was charged with "gross corruption, malfeasance of office, mismanagement of financial affairs, reckless litigation and general inability."[7] No public officer, the *Tribune* commented,

[3] *New York Tribune*, July 8, October 24, 1873.
[4] *New York Tribune*, September 10, 1873.
[5] *New York Tribune*, September 11, 1873.
[6] See Green's defense of his auditing procedures, Circular No. 7, March, 1873, Mayors Papers, Box 41.
[7] *New York Tribune*, October 9, 1873.

has within the past year made greater shipwreck of his popularity than Andrew H. Green.[8]

The mayor and comptroller had answers for all of these charges. They vigorously attacked "corrupt" claimants and defended their use of lobbyists. The legislature frequently adopted measures applying to New York City as a coherent unit yet the city as a whole was not represented. The mayor had difficulty simply finding out the contents of a bill under consideration. Havemeyer did not have control over the city delegation. He did not even have regular access to them. Under the previous Democratic regime the legislators had not been controlled by City Hall—they had been bought. The mayor and comptroller insisted that they could not be expected to serve as their own legislative representatives and at the same time perform their duties in the city. They could not be expected to "keep in touch" personally in two places at the same time.[9]

The fall election of 1873 with minor offices at stake wrote a dismal end to the organized reform movement which had overthrown Tweed. The mayor seemed almost to revel in his predicament as the return to the normal political pattern destroyed the underlying bases of his support. The Committee of Seventy voted to disband. Only twenty-nine members attended its final session. The Young Men's Municipal Reform Association which had canvassed from door to door for Havemeyer in 1872 was left at the end of 1873 with but 200 of its original 1500 members.[10]

The election was a regular Democratic victory, marked by a small vote and little enthusiasm. The major issue decided was the annexation of the western portion of Westchester into New York City, which was overwhelmingly approved over Havemeyer's

[8] New York Tribune, October 9, 1873.
[9] See Havemeyer's attack on a "knot of lawyers whose chief business is to ferret out flaws in laying assessments or awarding contracts for local improvements and whose income is chiefly derived from the spoils gathered in their piratical raids upon the treasury." Mayor of the City of New York, Message to the Common Council, January 19, 1874 (New York, 1874), pp. 33–35. Green's letter to Havemeyer, March 16, 1874, Mayors Papers, Box 41, explains the need for a representative in Albany.
[10] New York Tribune, October 22, November 4, 1873.

opposition. Promoters in the new area feared that they could not survive and prosper caught between the expanding giants of New York and Yonkers. Ever since 1869 when the Central Park Commission had been entrusted with planning their streets and public projects, the Westchester suburbs had been linked administratively to New York. The commission had worked slowly and developers moaned about the uncertainty which inhibited building and sales. Real estate owners in the northern part of Manhattan favored annexation because it would prevent the population from skipping over their area into the low-tax suburbs. The city had to move forward to catch up with the prospective movement of its middle class.[11]

In Havemeyer's terms, annexation was in the interests of "speculators on both sides of the Harlem River." The mayor believed in free trade, the free market place, and free and very limited government. The market linked New York to the outside world and would also hold the city together. Problems which could not be solved in the market place or by individuals acting separately should be dealt with in small communities where men knew and trusted each other. Havemeyer disparaged both the wisdom and the finality of the annexation of Westchester. "Municipal liberty," he contended, "was endangered by the prevailing tendency toward large and centralized schemes of local government. The principle of direct representation is everywhere giving place to a less responsible, because less definite, method of connecting the representative with the wants of a particular section of the community of whom he ought to be the legislative instrument." The natural boundary of New York was Manhattan Island. "With this Island," he pleaded, "which has constituted so long the City and County of New York, is associated all the traditions of our past history, and on and around it are all the conditions of our future greatness. Once entered on the mainland, where can we stop?"[12]

The major excitement of the 1873 election was generated by Tammany's charges against Police Commissioners Oliver Charlick

[11] Henry F. Spaulding to Mayor William Havemeyer, January 24, 1873, Mayors Papers, Box 215; George H. Foster to Havemeyer, Kingsbridge, April 13, 1874, Box 223.
[12] *Message, 1874*, pp. 40–41.

and Hugh Gardner. The two men, Kelly charged, had illegally removed several Tammany election inspectors on the eve of balloting.

The resolution of these charges and the reorganization of the Police Board is a long and dreary story in which, as frequently happened, the innocent bore the heaviest costs. The patrolmen were unpaid, garbage was left to rot in the street, and homes were unprotected. The story is significant only as a revelation of administrative confusion, the mayor's pride, and the pressures upon the Democratic leader. "I shall probably be the best abused man in New York," Havemeyer boasted in May, 1874, as he appointed an unknown twenty-eight-year-old to the Police Board. "I like that . . . I don't want to be praised, for then I think I am benefiting one party to the injury of another. I consult only the public good." [13]

If Havemeyer and Green had enjoyed greater expectations of aid and had attempted to encourage assistance they might have fared better. Tammany had initially acted with great friendliness to the new administration but had been alienated by the attack on the police justices. Kelly had maintained reasonably cordial relations with Green until the spring of 1874. The choice of Republican police justices and the threat to Tammany's ability to select election inspectors and to be represented on the Police Board made friendship almost impossible. Green further exacerbated relations by auditing all bills presented by the Sheriff's office, one of the few city patronage posts still in the hands of a loyal party man. The cut-back in public works and the discontinuance of public outdoor relief in July, 1874, made it difficult for district leaders to provide help to their constituents. [14]

The ward leaders were straining at the bit. The Committee on Organization had expanded its prerogatives during 1873. It claimed the right to reject the nomination offered by any local convention and to reorganize district delegations to the General Committee. The ward leaders, unhappy with this attempt to strengthen party discipline, charged that Kelly could neither provide for the party faithful nor for their lower-class public. The

[13] *New York Tribune*, May 8, 1874.
[14] *New York Tribune*, July 24, 27, 1874.

"Boss" had little choice but to break with Havemeyer and Green. Through the summer and fall of 1874 he traded bitter invectives and lawsuits with the Mayor, until Havemeyer's sudden death in November, put an end to the controversy.[15]

Attacked both from above and below, Kelly had to prove his loyalty to the political system upon which he depended. After a long delay, he endorsed James Hayes as Tammany candidate for city register. Hayes had been associated with the Tweed Board of Supervisors and had made a fortune out of politics. He was a classic local politician. His closest associate was John Morrissey, boxer, gambler, and ward politician—direct, outspoken, at once honest and violent. Kelly was reluctant to endorse Hayes for fear of hurting his state and local tickets. The nomination would lead to charges that Morrissey dominated the party. Kelly finally consented to Hayes in return for Morrissey's approval of William Wickham as the Tammany nominee for mayor.[16] Wickham was a diamond merchant and life-long Democrat who had been a member of the Committee of Seventy and O'Brien's Apollo Hall. He won handily, as did Samuel Jones Tilden, Democratic candidate for governor. The only surprise in the election was Hayes' defeat. He lost the new wards in Westchester and all but seven of the assembly districts on the island.

The Council of Political Reform at the end of 1874 issued a report on its first years of activity.[17] The report revealed the difficulties which the new city government would face. The president of the Council was William Webb, ship and house builder and owner, enemy of the Brooklyn Bridge and foe of the foreign steamship lines. "A Democratic-Republican government," Webb argued, "in a great city filled with citizens of diverse nationalities, and many of them not possessed of virtue or intelligence sufficient for self-government, is peculiarly exposed to official incompetence and corruption." The aims of the council were "honest, efficient and economical government." Almost every plan for improvement of the city appeared in his report as a "job," almost every politician

---

[15] *New York Tribune*, October 18, November 6 and 19, 1874.
[16] *New York Tribune*, October 10, 12, 1874.
[17] New York City Council of Political Reform, *Report for the Years 1872, '73 and '74* (New York, 1875).

a fraud and a thief. "The active political classes of the city," Webb contended, "are found among its adventurers, idlers and criminals, uneducated and without either moral or patriotic conviction . . . men who are champions and exponents of the very class against which society is organized to protect itself."

The Council's words indicated the distance which separated it from the poor and foreign of the city. Men in the far-off country did not simply have different values—they were without "moral or patriotic convictions," hardly real men at all. The Council's alarm was similar to the later panic in which many New Yorkers viewed the populist menace of the nineties as an attempt to subvert the American Republic.[18] Kansas and New York, Murray Hill and the Lower East Side, were connected by a limited communications network which could convey the state of prices but not a state of mind. The city, long before manufacturing firms complained of the symptoms, had become uncoupled.

[18] C. Vann Woodward, "The Populist Heritage and the Intellectual," *The American Scholar*, XIX (Winter, 1959), pp. 68–69.

ELEVEN

Structure, Not Party

A simple change of party or a bundle of campaign promises could not recouple or coordinate New York. The barriers to a collective policy based upon a deep-seated social consensus were too profound to be overcome by an isolated act of political will. The program of the Havemeyer administration was perpetuated and extended at the very moment when it appeared to have been defeated.

This basic continuity of policy was not apparent at the very beginning of 1875. As mayor-elect, Wickham toured the West Side, lending encouragement to hopes that he proposed to push development rapidly ahead. Once in office he appointed William R. Martin, president of the West Side Association, to the Parks Department, and met with Van Nort and Henry Stebbins and urged them to move ahead with new projects as rapidly as possible. The mayor suggested in his first official message that an active program of improvements, in addition to its other benefits, would employ men suffering from a business depression beyond their control. While, he insisted, the government did not have a responsibility to furnish jobs, in fact "in all large cities the public works provide for a portion of the community who are dependent principally upon them for employment. The suspension of the works is a serious misfortune to those so dependent." Since the unemployed desired jobs and not charity and their labor contributed to the wealth of the city they ought to be given work "when it is practicable to do so." [1]

[1] *New York Tribune*, November 30, 1874, January 8, 1875; William Wickham, Mayor of the City of New York, *Message to the Common Council, Board of Aldermen, January 4, 1875* (New York, 1875), pp. 22–23.

114

Uptown real estate owners smiled. Improvements in the new areas, they insisted, benefited the whole city. Under Havemeyer and Green, one developer wrote the mayor, real estate had "gone to the dogs." With Wickham and Martin in office, revival was assured.[2]

Green vehemently opposed the new direction. "The public interests," he contended on February 15, "would be better served by devoting such moneys as the city has to expend to the repair and improvement of the streets in the lower part of the city, now in such bad condition, and which are needed for daily use by throngs of people, and which are a constant necessity for the movement of persons and property." The better part of the uptown project, he argued, were of "no present utility." He urged the Board of Estimate and Apportionment to put every possible obstacle in the way of further uptown appropriations.

Martin appealed to downtown pocketbooks. The city, he insisted, had been amply rewarded for everything it had spent uptown. The value of property had increased and tax revenues had been correspondingly swollen. He estimated the cost to the public treasury of completing the work already authorized or planned at about $7,500,000. An additional $12,000,000 would have to be assessed upon property holders for street openings and improvements. "Since the amount of annual expenditure cannot be diminished," he reasoned, "the only way to relieve the burden of the city debt was to increase the value of property on the tax rolls. During the previous three years, uptown valuations had gone up "as if this had been a season of prosperity," while downtown valuations had remained unchanged. "But there must be some basis for such an increase," he concluded, "if it is to be continued." The prosecution of these public improvements will supply it at a small expense to the downtown property owner. "It is the most effectual means to save him from the like increase of taxation, and to furnish a larger amount of property on which taxation is laid, and thus lighten the burden."[3]

[2] A. J. Land to Wickham, Brooklyn, January 2, 1875, Mayors Papers, Box 224.
[3] William R. Martin, *A Communication Relative to the Prosecution of Public Improvements in this City* (New York, 1875), pp. 21–35.

Rather than cut back on public planning and development, Martin insisted on the immediate need to complete plans for the section of Manhattan above 155th Street and the new wards of Westchester. He met with little success. In 1876 and 1877 he was still making the same demands, pleading the same case he had urged in 1875.

The most important result of his efforts was the revision of plans for Riverdale in the westernmost portion of the new wards. The street map prepared for the region in 1873 extended a slightly modified gridiron across the hills. At Martin's urging, Frederick Olmsted prepared a new design for a terraced suburb which was accepted by the commission over Commissioner Henry Stebbin's vigorous opposition in April, 1877. The design integrated shops and schools, public gardens and rapid transit facilities. It was intended, Olmsted said, for a walking and not a "heavy teaming" population. A city, like a house, he argued, has many rooms. The attempt to make every section equally convenient for every prospective user ended only with a cluster of areas which were "equally inconvenient." Planning, Olmsted conceded, required forecasting the future. Prediction was difficult but the alternative was chaos. New York, he lectured, would have its suburbs. "It remains a question whether they shall be formed by a co-operation of public and private work, or by private enterprise in making the best of unsuitable public arrangements." [4]

Shortly after the adoption of his Riverdale design, Olmsted lost his position as chief landscape architect of the Department of Parks and his street plan remained an isolated remnant of a total neighborhood design. His broader hopes for the new wards were not realized. The ultimate victory remained with Stebbins, who protested that he did not understand Olmsted's concern for aesthetic standards and the establishment of a community separated from the hurly-burly of city life. The city, he insisted, was in a constant state of movement and change. It was unwise to impose a

---

[4] "Report of the Landscape Architect and the Civil and Topographical Engineer Accompanying a plan for laying out that part of the Twenty-fourth Ward Lying West of Riverdale Road," *Minutes of Proceedings of the Board of Commissioners of Public Parks for the Year Ending April 30, 1877* (New York, 1877), Document 72, pp. 8–10, 14–18.

rigid design upon any region. "Custom, convenience, and utility in their thousand varying aptitudes and relationships," have seized upon the gridiron as the model of flexibility. After all, Stebbins concluded, the old plan allowed for fine *individual* villa sites.[5]

There was an ironic logic in the orientation of political debate. The discussion within the Parks Department about the planning of Riverdale directly focused on the major issues of the city's character and future. The discussion was not part of a general public confrontation of these issues. It was, indeed, hardly publicized at all. Public debate focused so heavily on the costs of new projects—and on projects which had readily defined price tags attached to them—that it could not usually come to grips with the alternatives defined in the exchange between Olmsted and Stebbins.

The alternatives phrased by Green and Martin were debated. Indeed, they represent the classic positions in the history of American urban and continental expansion. The victory in New York and in the nation lay with men who stood somewhere between the two extremes. The cities and the nation grew outward without waiting for improvement of the old settlement. The public did not, however, expend the funds to plan and develop the new regions so that their residents intimately sensed their vital relationship to the old core. Metropolises grew without metropolitans, regions without regionalists.

The unfolding of this "compromise," (was it worse than either of the two alternatives?) began quickly in New York. The close calculation of costs and immediate rather than long-term benefits loomed larger and larger in Mayor Wickham's mind as he was educated in office. The early hopes which he raised were never fulfilled.

As early as March 18, 1875, he wrote a letter to the Board of Aldermen which pleased Green enormously. The burden of taxes upon property owners was so heavy, he contended, that the city's indebtedness could not be increased safely. Department heads should be clearly and definitively forbidden to spend more money than had been legally authorized. The laws, dating from the

---

[5] *Ibid.*, Document 74, pp. 2–12.

Tweed era, which provided for increased borrowing should be repealed. "Our progress in the future," he wrote, "should be determined by our ability to meet our obligations in the past; and only in the ratio in which we actually pay for public improvements already executed or undertaken should we proceed with new enterprises which require further expenditure." He proposed a limit of $15,000,000 on the issuance of bonds to cover unpaid assessments. The city indebtedness on this account was then more than $21,000,000. Finally, Wickham proposed a central agency controlling and planning city improvements.

On the very same day, Green sent a letter to the legislature which outlined the measures necessary to put city affairs on a basis satisfactory to the "substantial portion of the citizens." Expenses must be reduced, unauthorized spending prohibited, and the Tweed-era borrowing laws repealed. The use of assessment bonds should be stringently curtailed. The city, he argued, was a factor raising money on its own credit to pay for works executed for private benefit. "The substantial people," he repeated with an obvious fondness for the phrase, were determined to expel the "sinecurists and corruptionists" from the city government; to prevent "uptown corner lot speculators," from mortgaging the "substance of the community in aid of visionary schemes of self-interest," and to place the affairs of the city "on the solid foundations of order and integrity from whence alone can proceed the upbuilding of substantial prosperity."

Later in the year Green clarified the meaning of the phrase, "substantial people." Downtown property owners, he contended, were no longer satisfied to spend millions for "untimely improvements in waste places," while the busy avenues of the old settlement were crowded and out of repair and children roamed the streets because there was not enough money for schoolhouses to accomodate them.[6]

The basic argreement between Green and Wickham apparent in these two letters was obscured by quarrels over details of administration and by jockeying for control of new programs proposed in the legislature. Green insisted that the mayor personally

---

[6] Green to Wickham, October 9, 1875, Mayors Papers, Box 422.

sign every warrant for city payments. Wickham refused and pay-rolls were shipped back and forth from one office to another accompanied by increasingly nasty notes. As early as February, Wickham angrily returned a letter from Green. "I cannot entertain or receive such a communication from a subordinate officer," he insisted.[7]

Green, in return, argued that he was attacking the most fundamental problem of city government, administrative supervision and control. The Department of Public Works, he pointed out in the course of a dispute in October and November, let out work on ninety-three contracts. Several more projects were undertaken by its own laborers. Public works were scattered over a broad area and could not be personally supervised by the superintendent. His immediate subordinates and his corps of forty inspectors were recruited for their political virtues and not their knowledge of construction. Even if the top bureaucrats had been experts, the problems of supervision would have been enormous since the turn-over of the labor force was so high. Under these conditions, Green asserted, a change in the basis of recruitment was absolutely necessary. Until this was accomplished, however, the mayor and department heads must check each expenditure in order to maintain the closest possible control over their agencies.[8]

Wickham vigorously contested Green's demands upon his time, but was acutely aware of the fundamental administrative problems which bedeviled the comptroller. He frequently learned about essential policy decisions when they were publicized in the press or attacked by critics. "I've been told," he wrote to Henry Stebbins in October, "that the Park Department has recently begun work on Riverside Park." Wickham had been "told" by Green the previous day and was at a loss for information.[9]

The mayor indicted other administrators for faults of method. He accused the fire commissioners held over from Havemeyer's term of allowing employees to remain idle, duplicating purchases,

---

[7] Wickham to Green, February 5, 1875, Mayors Papers, Letter Book, January, 1875-May, 1876.

[8] Green to Wickham, November 15, 1875, Mayors Papers, Box 422.

[9] Wickham to Henry Stebbins, October 11, 1875, Mayors Papers, Letter Book, January, 1875-May, 1876.

failing to keep proper records and holding interests in supply companies. He charged the police commissioners with similar faults and asked that they be removed from office. Commissioner Henry Smith, protesting the charges, confirmed Green's analysis of the problems of city government but challenged his prescription. Smith found on taking office a loosely organized force of 2400 men. The responsibility of superior officers, he said, was "too remote and vague for the purposes of good discipline." The bases of recruitment and formal organization had to be changed before any single man could hope to "control" the force or insist upon the rules.[10]

Smith suggested a fundamental difficulty in changing New York's government. The demand to stop wrong-doing immediately and the tactics of fundamental administrative reform were different and even conflicting.

The administrative quarrel between Wickham and Green was exacerbated in Albany. Wickham's friends warned him that Green's every effort was being used to "destroy your power," and to heap disgrace upon the Democratic Party. Green's direct memorials to the legislature, Wickham stormed, are "subversive of every principle of good and responsible government."[11]

The conflict between the two men centered around bills to reorganize the city government and to initiate two important new programs. The legislature, besieged by a host of special claims for repaving, authorized the city spend up to $500,000 annually for new pavements. Urged on by the fire insurance companies, it also appropriated $1,500,000 for a new water reservoir.

A legislative mandate did not mean that work was actually begun. The spirits of economy and party contrived to produce further delay. The Board of Estimate and Apportionment did not allocate a single dollar for repavement in fixing the budget for 1876. At the beginning of 1875, George Van Nort was replaced by a Democrat, General Fitz John Porter, as public works commissioner. The Republicans on the Board of Aldermen, probably as anxious to deprive the Democrats of patronage as they were

[10] *City Record,* February 3, 1875.
[11] Wickham to Green, March 19, 1875, Mayors Papers, Letter Book, January, 1875-May, 1876.

The Docks, 1869: Too big a problem for a divided city. *Historical Pictures Service—Chicago*

for economy, insisted that future public works should be executed by contract and not by city-hired day laborers. The Democrats refused to allocate funds under these conditions and no allowance was made for the new water works.[12]

Strong party government, so often denounced by reformers as the death of the city, seemed to be the basic requirement for vigorous public action. Some improvement was made at the end of the decade in the pavement of downtown business streets and the new reservoir was eventually built. The city failed to either run ahead of its own need for water or to solve the problem of movement in its business areas.

The waterfront, uniformly the object of merchant despair, was not rebuilt. The concrete bulkheads and piers constructed on the "cheap" plan adopted by the dock commissioners in 1874, showed signs of crumbling in 1875. The commissioners promised a new beginning, but it was not as easy to take the initiative in the second half of the decade as it had been in the first. Work was crippled by constant changes in personnel. Six different administrative boards and three different chief engineers were charged with responsibility for the docks between 1870 and 1877.[13] The uncertainties of administration, compounding the uncertainties of the market, increased costs. In 1875, for example, the commissioners were accused of storing an excessive number of dock piles. They defended themselves vigorously, describing how work in the past had been periodically halted by the need to wait for complex authorizations for purchases and reliance on immediately available supplies. It was absolutely necessary, they argued, to hold generous inventories in readiness for construction to reduce the costs of administrative and market delay.[14]

The reconstruction of the waterfront was frustrated by divisions within the commercial community and by the opposition of

[12] *New York Tribune,* October 1, 1875; Department of Public Works, *Report for the Quarter Ending December 31, 1876* (New York, 1877), p. 6.
[13] Eugene K. Lynch, *Facts Relating to the Department of Docks of the City of New York and Reasons for Its Continuance As a Separate Department of the City Government* (New York, 1877), pp. 4–5, 8.
[14] "Defense of Commissioners Westervelt and Budd," February 12, 1875, Mayors Papers, Box 63.

the owners of waterfront property. In the last three years of the decade, the income of the hobbled Dock Commission exceeded its expenditures by nearly $900,000. Salem Wales, president of the commission, begged to be freed from the "persistent opposition of reform and taxpaying associations," to every new project of improvement.[15]

The dock commissioners attributed their inability to break through these conflicting interests to shape an effective public policy to a general suspicion of politicians. City ownership of waterfront property was still "so patchy," the commissioners said in 1879, that comprehensive reconstruction of the docks would require either large purchases or "co-operative endeavor." Great new purchases were unlikely, they thought, since people seemed increasingly to feel "that large property interests are not usually well managed by public officers, or, at best, that the result of such management cannot, as a rule, compare favorably with the result obtained by prudent men managing their own." [16] The shift from public to private initiative was, more than anything else, simply a reduction in the scale and complexity of the enterprise to be managed.

The hopes of the early seventies for rapid transportation within the city were not frustrated in the same way as was the vision of a new waterfront. Rapid transportation survived because the public costs were severely reduced and private capitalists, acting in a new field, were encouraged to build on a broad scale. The legislative settlement which opened the way for the construction of the elevated roads along Sixth and Ninth Avenues was reached in 1875. The isolated grandeur of this achievement in transportation created a new urban frontier. Uptown development in Manhattan ground to a halt after the middle of the decade. The new wards of the Bronx were still asking for a firm decision on a street plan in 1879. As on the Great Plains, the means of transportation reached out beyond the area which men imaginatively related

---

[15] "Suggestions about the Department of Docks, Remarks Made by Mr. Wales, President of the Department of Docks, at the Conference Held at the Mayor's Office, February 10, 1877," Mayors Papers, Box 62.
[16] Department of Docks, *Ninth Annual Report for the Year Ending April 30, 1879* (New York, 1879), p. 20.

to their own interests and for which they could plan. "One might as well move to Minnesota as to the top of Manhattan," Henry James' Marian Almond avowed.[17] The result of this gap between the broad scope of the physical means of transportation and the narrow circle of imagination and information was the same in the city as on the plains: an urban frontier of shanty rows, dusty roads and a rigid perpetuation of old patterns.[18]

The opposition to the construction of rapid transit lines prior to 1875 came principally from three sources: the street railway companies, Cornelius Vanderbilt, and a group of downtown real estate owners led by A. T. Stewart. Stewart was particularly anxious to keep the prime Broadway route free of mass transit facilities. The successful 1875 bill which broke this opposing coalition was sponsored by Tilden himself. The mayor, on petition of property owners, was empowered to appoint a commission to map out a rapid transit system and to offer franchises to private entrepreneurs. Stewart and Vanderbilt were satisfied by provisions of the law which explicitly prohibited the construction of lines along Fourth Avenue above the 42nd Street terminal of the Central and along Broadway and Fifth Avenue below 59th Street.

The commission's decisions were bound to favor the two major corporations that already had franchises to build elevated lines, the Gilbert and the New York Elevated. These were the only lines which would not require the consent of adjoining property owners before they could be built. The limit which the commission was able to place on the number of lines seemed to insure the profitability of the projected roads. The commissioners prided themselves on the hope that they had prepared the final solution to a long-standing and troublesome problem.[19]

The roads received no public assistance other than the free use of the streets. This grant of the streets challenged the vested

---

[17] Henry James, *Washington Square*, in William Phillips, ed., *Great American Short Novels* (New York: Dial Press, 1946), p. 99.
[18] The course of development is illustrated in a useful supplement published by the *Real Estate Record and Builders Guide*, LIII (May 12, 1894) entitled "A History of Real Estate, Building, Architecture in New York City, 1868–1893."
[19] James Blaine Walker, *Fifty Years of Rapid Transit, 1864 to 1917* (New York: Law Printing Co., 1918), pp. 104–114.

interests of both streetcar companies and adjoining owners. They challenged the constitutionality of the act and demanded compensation for the losses they would incur with the construction of the els.

William Evarts, soon to take up the post of United States secretary of state, was the chief attorney for the property owners. He conceded that the public's right to rapid transit preceded the rights of property. The state could grant the roads the privilege of eminent domain. The public interest did not, however, precede the individual's claim upon the law to protect his private property. Private rights had been violated by empowering the companies to use the public streets without compensation to the owners of abutting property. The city, he argued, had implicitly pledged itself to maintain the through way. That pledge was as much violated by constructing an elevated railroad as by erecting a building in the middle of a street. The court, he urged, should not hesitate to declare the Rapid Transit Act unconstitutional. In the recent past, he contended, the judiciary had wisely expanded the scope of its judgments, protecting primary individual rights by restricting legislatures.[20]

Evarts' arguments were rejected. In September, 1877, the New York Court of Appeals upheld the constitutionality of the Rapid Transit Act in two parallel cases. In the Gilbert suit, Chief Justice Sanford Church, speaking for the majority, clung to accepted judicial doctrine which gave a strong presumption of constitutionality to the legislative will. "An adverse doubtful construction," he cautioned, "is not sufficient to condemn an act." The courts, he contended, should refrain from precious and narrow interpretations of the constitution which deprived the legislature of the ability to meet public needs." Over the protests of three judges who agreed with Evarts, the court dodged the issue of the rights of property owners to compensation. This evasive decision came back to haunt the elevated lines in the 1880's.[21]

Compare the decision to ignore vested rights in the construction of the rapid transit lines with the careful concern for vested rights exhibited by the Central Park Commission in the 1860's. Green had broached the possibility of facing the houses in the new areas around central lawns in order to integrate neighborhoods. He rejected the idea as a costly and unpopular invasion of the established claims of property owners. The claims were ignored in the building of the rapid transit lines for the same reasons that they were respected on the West Side. Evarts' argument would have placed an enormous barrier to movement and change in a restless city.

Giving the els free use of the streets was the only public assistance possible in the middle of the seventies. The demand for economy, a nagging exhortation in 1874, was the governing premise of public policy in 1875. Mayor Wickham and the new Democratic commissioner of public works, Fitz John Porter, announced in May that the wages of unskilled laborers would be cut from a minimum of twenty-five cents down to twenty cents an hour. The reduction, they argued, would bring city wages into line with those paid by private employers.[22]

Laborers, the aldermen who depended upon the patronage of Porter's department, and Tammany Hall all protested vehemently but unsuccessfully. William Martin, hoping to enlist lower-class support for his own expansionist policies, argued that government had a special obligation to pay a living wage, even if it was above the going rate. Wickham stood firm and protested rather plaintively that he was "at a loss to perceive how prices of labor, any more than prices of commodities, can be regulated by Legislation—or otherwise than by the laws of supply and demand which make market rates."[23]

The reductions precipitated a major dispute over the proper role of government in the economy. A group of men concerned with good government and representing, as they said, the ag-

---

[22] *New York Tribune*, May 29, 1875.
[23] *A True Statement of the Position of Tammany Hall on the Labor Question*, October 25, 1875 (New York, 1875); *New York Tribune*, June 5, 1875; Wickham to Hamilton Fish, Jr., January 6, 1876, Mayors Papers, Letter Book, January, 1875-May, 1876.

grieved taxpayers of the city, charged Martin and one of his fellow commissioners, Joseph J. O'Donohue, with official turpitude. The beleaguered commissioners responded with an attack upon the market mechanism and a renewed call for public works. "We would rather be found urging the judicious program of public improvements," they boasted, than "to sit in the parlor of the Union League Club, pandering to the prejudices of the wealthy who want their taxes reduced, and have so little wisdom as to think they promote their object by enforcing the theories of economy, from which the laws of the state protect them, against the laboring class, so as to increase their suffering and distress." The rich were protected with tariffs, combinations, and the manipulation of money. The poor enjoyed only the "sacrificial side of public retrenchment."[24]

The petitioners responded firmly. Twenty thousand city taxpayers, they said, demanded the reduction. "The debt of the city is unprecedented," Dexter Hawkins proclaimed. "There is nothing like it in the history of the world." The payment of two dollars a day to park laborers was a "breach of faith" and "a want of business discretion." Martin's wage theories, Dorman Eaton concluded, were "romantic." Business and government were both ruled by the iron law of wages.[25]

The debate was resolved with an ironic twist which, I suspect, is characteristic of American politics. Martin and O'Donohue retained their jobs; Fitz John Porter, who was associated in the popular mind with the reduction, lost his. The wage cut was not rescinded. The rule of the market was preserved.

The clamor for economy stemmed from the general business depression which began to effect real estate seriously in the fall of 1874. The value of lots declined 25 to 40 per cent. There was a sharp rise in the number of real estate foreclosures, leaving unwanted foreclosed property in the hands of insurance and trust companies and savings banks. Mutual Life, for example, held

[24] William Martin and Joseph J. O'Donohue to Wickham, December 1, 1876, Mayors Papers, Box 347.
[25] "Stenographic Minutes of Hearing Before the Mayor in the Matter of Charges Against Commissioners Martin and O'Donohue," Mayors Papers, Box 347.

$30,000,000 in city mortgages. Foreclosed land, by 1876, was costing the firm $190,000 annually in local taxes. The company's annual report issued on January 1, 1876 denounced the "reckless course taken by cities and towns during and immediately after the war, in projecting and carrying out premature improvements in opening streets, sewerage, paving and other similar enterprises." The inhabitants had been burdened by liabilities which were "exceedingly oppressive and in many cases ruinous." [26]

The depression led many groups in the city to try to shift the tax burden off their own shoulders. As they maneuvered for advantages, the entire system of taxation was opened to critical examination. A small group of tax reformers urged thorough tax revision. This group included George Andrews, who in addition to his duties as a city commissioner of taxes and assessments was a director of the Mutual Life Insurance Company; James Briggs, a member of the State Board of Equalization; and David A. Wells, the free trade economist. In a series of places, and with growing insistence after 1875, they argued essentially the same position. All levies on personal property should be abolished and real estate should be relieved of the burden of all, or nearly all, state taxes. Corporations should be exempt from local taxes in return for payment of a state corporation tax. The value of real estate should be determined by state and not by local assessors. [27]

The tax reformers hoped to rationalize the financial bases of state and local government. The existing tax system, they argued, was insensitive to changes in current income and was inadequate

[26] *Real Estate Record and Builder's Guide*, LIII (May 12, 1894), p. 37; Mutual Life Insurance Company of New York, *Thirty-third Annual Report, January 1, 1876* (New York, 1876); Frederick S. Winston, president of the Mutual Life Insurance Company, *Facts and Observations as to Financial and Business Affairs Generally and their Influence on the Investments and Condition of the Company, Addressed to the Committee on Finance and Board of Trustees for their Consideration and Action, July, 1876* (New York, 1876), pp. 3–6.

[27] The literature on tax reform is reviewed in David Wells, "The Reform of Local Taxation," *North American Review*, CXXII (April, 1876), pp. 357–403. See also *Real Estate Record and Builder's Guide*, XII (December 21, 1878), pp. 1023–1025 and the Commissioners of Taxes and Assessments, *Taxes and Assessments, Report of the Commissioners, 1876* (New York, 1876), pp. 23–52 and *1877* (New York, 1877), pp. 22–23.

to meet new demands upon the public treasury. Heavy reliance upon the real estate tax was costly to the whole society because it raised the price of urban housing and helped to engender the shoddy building and congestion for which New York paid so dearly.

Change in the tax system emerged slowly from a complex and bitter fight between contending interests which raged across the legislative halls, executive offices and courts of the city, state, and nation. The reformers encountered almost no success in the seventies for much the same reasons as similar proposals in other areas were rejected. The beneficiaries of decentralization, no matter how much they complained, thought they could maximize their benefits in a loosely coordinated, competitive system. Andrews, for example, justified his proposals, at least in part, as a way of successfully taxing the railroads. But real estate owners were not sure that the proposals were to their benefit. With state taxes falling and personal property already evading the conveniently averted glance of the assessor, real estate did not seem to have anything to gain from revision. The *Real Estate Record* angrily rejected the arguments for reform and insisted that the city and state claim additional revenues by imposing heavy taxes on the franchises of ferry and street railway companies.[28]

The conditions which underlay the basic "compromise" in development were thus sharply phrased in the depression of the seventies: administrative uncoupling, public division, and a restricted and inflexible tax base. Governor Tilden, sensitive to these conditions, appointed a special commission to study the "decay of municipal government." The commission was to be chaired by William Evarts and included among others E. L. Godkin, editor of the *Nation*, and Simon Sterne, a vigorous reforming lawyer and publicist. Tilden suggested to the commission that it draft a general law for cities, which would place greater authority in the hands of taxpayers. They might be given special powers to check expenditures and curb delinquent officials. They might even undertake to execute public works themselves. "There is no rea-

---

[28] *Real Estate Record and Builder's Guide*, XIX (May 26, 1877), pp. 419–421, and (June 23, 1877), pp. 499–500. Most historical treatments of the era of laissez-faire ignore the critical dimension of the fiscal bases of government.

son," the governor said, "why the persons taxable for the improvement of a street should not be allowed to associate and by their agents execute the work for which they pay." [29]

Tilden's message was a devastating rejection of the hopes for public action which had been raised in the sixties. It may be that men raised in the country or in small towns expect more of voluntary associations than men who are city-bred. Tilden, Tweed had once laughed, was the leader of the "cheese-press and hay-loft Democracy." [30]

While the old boss, the symbol of centralization, rested (too comfortably some said) in prison, New York explored the possibilities of a return to decentralization and the limitation of political participation.

[29] Charles Z. Lincoln, ed., *Messages From the Governors of the State of New York* (Albany: J. B. Lyon, 1909), VI, pp. 825–844.
[30] Alexander C. Flick, *Samuel Jones Tilden* (New York: Dodd, Mead, 1939), p. 200.

TWELVE

The Rejection of Kelly

The appointment of the Tilden Commission heralded the collapse of the social communication upon which Tweed had rested his power. The collapse came, ironically, at the moment when the Irish wanted most desperately to share both the values and the rewards of respectable society.

Kelly worked assiduously in 1875 to strengthen the central direction of the Democratic party at the expense of the ward "bosses." The Committee on Organization ruled in March that, in the future, patronage would be distributed through the general committee of each assembly district and not through individual leaders. The leaders charged that they were being forced to share with the "swallow-tail Democracy," which had no legitimate claim upon the spoils of party warfare.[1]

Kelly instituted a series of meetings between the Committee on Organization and Democratic city representatives in Albany to discuss issues and decide on uniform policies.[2] The city legislative delegation throughout the decade was remarkably unstable. The twenty-five Senate seats from New York in the years between 1870 and 1879 were filled by 22 different senators; the 211 places in the lower house by 164 different assemblymen. The results of the constant turnover in personnel were gross mistakes in the drafting of legislation and an irresponsible and undisciplined sensitivity to special private claims. The instability in the legislative delegation reflected not merely the low prestige of political office, but the unsettled distribution of power in a rapidly growing

---

[1] *New York Tribune*, March 15, 1875.
[2] *New York Tribune*, February 8, 1875.

city. Only a few well-to-do Republican enclaves and the older downtown tenement districts sent representatives back year-after-year. Kelly's meetings promised responsible party discipline and a settled policy.

The centralization of power engendered criticism. Assemblymen lamented that they, and not the Committee on Organization, had been elected by the people and should have the use of patronage. Party workers charged that the Manhattan Club composed of the social elite of the Democratic Party, received all the valuable prizes and only scraps were left for the hard-working party faithful. Morrissey paraded along Madison Square in dinner dress with a French dictionary under his arm. He was going to see the mayor to ask for office, he explained, and no one could get an appointment unless he wore kid gloves and spoke French.[3]

The criticism from "above" was more important than the carping from "below." Kelly's leadership was born in the reform reaction against Tweed and he remained a child of reform, searching for respectability and approval. He represented a new Irish middle class committed to the thoroughly American idea that good hard work would be rewarded by success. If this new middle class was to slip effortlessly into the society of the older residents of the city, Kelly and his generation had to be accommodated and encouraged.

The barriers to integration were enormous. The Irish had a strong sense of personal loyalty and a dependence on tribal hierarchies scorned by the native Americans. The Irish prided themselves on their devotion to the city, yet they suspected many of its impersonal, antitraditional ways. They were convinced of the importance of working through channels and demanded only that the men they respected at the top, acknowledge their dependence on the followers below.[4]

The cluster of Irish attitudes towards authority reflected both a different cultural tradition and the characteristic outlook of men

---

[3] *New York Tribune,* March 26, 1875.
[4] Daniel P. Moynihan, "When the Irish Ran New York," *Reporter,* XXIV (June 8, 1961), pp. 32–34, may stretch the definition a bit too far in calling the Irish party organization, "bureaucratic." The hierarchy was closer to a system of highly developed subinfeudation.

in all societies who enjoy only a limited acquaintance with the world outside of their own immediate milieu. In New York in the seventies, the suspicion of strangers and the resistance to accommodation which was expected at the bottom of society, appeared also at the very top. Barriers to communication blocked the flow of information which would have made the world that was just around the corner real and human. Distance encouraged men to think in stereotypes and to imagine that society was endangered by vast conspiracies. The Irishmen in Thomas Nast's cartoons for *Harper's Weekly* were uniformly ape-like. "The average Catholic Irishman of the first generation, as represented in this Assembly," Theodore Roosevelt wrote in his legislative diary in 1882, "is a low, venal, corrupt and unintelligent brute." [5]

The obstacles to integration were great, but Tilden in 1872 had argued that they were not insurmountable. The bottom was rising, he said. The Negro was free, immigrants filled the land, and great cities challenged the traditional image of the good life. "This is the state of things. Who could alter it if he would? Who dare say that, on the whole, he would alter it if he could?" The task then, he concluded, was to avoid civil and social revolution and "work out as best we may the problems of self-government formed on equal and universal suffrage." [6]

Tilden complicated this difficult task in 1875 by quarreling with Kelly. The issue between them was the retention of Green as comptroller. The political result of the demand for economy was the aggravation of the tension between the "good government men" and the new Irish leadership.

Abram Hewitt begged Tilden to come to terms with the city leader. Kelly, Hewitt reported, was ready to meet Tilden's views on every point except the retention of Green. Hewitt conceded that the Governor could not openly abandon Green, but he might encourage the comptroller to place his resignation in Tilden's hands to be used "only when a successor satisfactory to you and to Kelly can be agreed." Failure to compromise, he warned, would

---

[5] Elting E. Morison, ed., *The Letters of Theodore Roosevelt* (Cambridge: Harvard University Press, 1951), II, p. 1470.
[6] John Bigelow, ed., *Letters and Literary Memorials of Samuel J. Tilden* (New York: Harper, 1908), I, pp. 315–318.

result in the destruction of the party machinery essential to Til-den's political success. Hewitt described a conversation with Green in which the comptroller showed a complete inability to under-stand "the intense disgust with which he is regarded by the Tam-many organization." He thought his position "impregnable," and suggested that the General Committee might be persuaded to endorse him. "I told him very frankly," Hewitt wrote, "that it would be destruction to those who are really his friends to make any such issue in the Committee. Your position and character will be with me the first consideration," Hewitt concluded, "and after that it seems to me that Kelly's position should be made as easy for him as the circumstances will admit." [7]

Samuel Barlow, a corporation attorney who was Tilden's political confidant, endorsed a similar position. The Governor could enter the Democratic National Convention in 1876 with a hope of being nominated for president only if he enjoyed the complete support of the New York delegation. Green, Barlow said, incited unnecessary quarrels with men anxious to be Tilden's allies, and converted them into aggressive enemies. "For such labors, Green seems to have been specially created . . ." [8]

Tilden received very different advice from other New Yorkers. Charles O'Conor asked him to scorn Wickham and his "concern for our friends." Dwight Townsend, former Democratic congressman and a founder of the Equitable Life Assurance Com-pany, reported that the "financial interests" were satisfied with Green. Certainly, the comptroller lacked "urbanity,'" but, Town-send observed, "perhaps if he possessed it he would not be as resolute." William A. Booth asked Tilden to stand by Green. Things have been going from "bad to worse" in the last few months, he complained. [9]

Tilden silently supported the comptroller at the cost of Kelly's friendship. The city leader could hardly afford to lose political allies. Aggrieved local politicians whom he had offended through his tactics of centralization clustered around Morrissey. The fiery

[7] Hewitt to Tilden, New York, February 23, 1875, Tilden Papers.
[8] Barlow to Tilden, New York, April 20, 1875, Tilden Papers.
[9] O'Conor to Tilden, New York, February 11, 1875; Townsend to Tilden, New York, March 10, 1875 and Booth to Tilden, New York, February 4, 1875, Tilden Papers.

gambler was expelled from the party in July, 1875, and several districts were reorganized. He promised revenge. Kelly was all right "until success made him wild," Morrissey told reporters. He had "turned on every man in Tammany Hall who helped to make him what he is and assisted in putting him in the front," he complained. "You can't run a political organization without working men in it and these must be taken care of if you want to keep them in it. A politician can no more ignore his organization and party than a man can snub his creditor. That's what Kelly and Wickham are doing," he warned, "and there will be a foreclosure soon. . . ."[10]

Kelly protested that he bore Morrissey no personal grudge, but that the ex-boxer and gambler's past life and business "rendered him odious to many in the Tammany organization and repelled many other good Democrats who would not affiliate with it so long as he held a prominent position and claimed to influence the action of the Tammany Hall General Committee and had a voice in the making of nominations."[11]

Morrissey and his friends had an ideal campaign issue. He blamed the cut in wages on Kelly. The Tammany leader and the General Committee denied the charge, and protested that they had counselled against it. The wage reduction refuted the contention that Kelly dictated municipal policy.

Morrissey found allies. Many German Democrats were unhappy with the Irish leadership. The president of the German American Independent Citizens Association offered to form a coalition against Tammany. "Tammany Hall," the association resolved, "ruled as it is by the will of a few, subject to a discipline akin to that of a military organization and subject to influences brought to bear in favor of sects or nationalities is frought with the greatest danger; it is a menace to our free institutions; is capable of being manipulated in the interest of fraud and corruption, contaminating even state and national politics." [12]

The Republicans agreed to a common front against Tammany. The opposition coalition was no more united on a single policy

[10] *New York Tribune*, July 24, 1875.
[11] *New York Tribune*, July 26, 1875.
[12] *New York Tribune*, October 2, 1875.

than was the regular party. It included men who opposed the wage reduction and those who favored it, those who were staunch supporters of Tilden and those who were indifferent to his reform work. Though it might create later difficulties in the process of governing, the diversity of views was immediately advantageous. The regular Democratic state ticket carried New York City by about 30,000 votes, but the local Tammany slate was badly beaten. Ten Republican, three Anti-Tammany and eight Tammany assemblymen were elected. Four of the five Senate seats in the city were taken by the Republican-Anti-Tammany coalition. Morrissey carried Tweed's old senate district. All of the Tammany judges were defeated.

Kelly was obviously stunned. He berated the press for hammering at his one-man power while ignoring the quality of his candidates. He had pledged his support for Tilden's reform of the administration of the Erie Canal and had spoken emphatically of the need to elevate the character of the municipal judiciary. Tammany's nominees for the bench had been widely praised. The Democratic leader denounced the introduction of the wage issue. The Democracy he contended, "had never attempted to raise one class of people as against another." "Contentment amongst the working class," another Tammany speaker insisted, "was a guaranty of peace and order in the community." "We have done everything we could," Kelly declared, "to reform the immense abuses that exist in this city." [13]

The defeat had to be softened. Kelly wrote Tilden on November 20 to affirm his wholehearted agreement with the Governor's hard money views. He dismissed Democratic losses in Ohio and Pennsylvania as of only "passing importance." Would the Governor, he asked, like to become a member of Tammany Hall?[14]

The letter was a politic disguise for Kelly's real exasperation. He felt that he had been slighted during the campaign and could not but resent the excuse that Tilden's support for Tammany would have hurt the state ticket. While he would not obstruct the governor's political plans, he told James Sinnott, Tilden's friend and Democratic judicial candidate, in February, 1876, he had no

[13] *New York Tribune,* November 5, 1875.
[14] Kelly to Tilden, New York, November 20, 1875, Tilden Papers.

interest in aiding them. Francis Kernan, the Utica Catholic who entered the United States Senate in 1875 on the heels of the Democratic state victory, visited New York to attempt a reconciliation, without success. Only Tilden could offer the prestige and the support which would conciliate the Tammany leader.[15]

Dr. Thomas Cottman, in a letter to Tilden, offered a revealing analysis of the differences which divided the Democracy. "Success with Tammany as at present organized," he wrote, "is entirely out of the question . . . John Kelly as chief with Ned Gale, Tom Boize, Frank Spinola, Billy Boyd and the like as chief counsel, will inevitably bring disaster upon the party . . . I would in no wise deprecate Mr. Kelly, whom I regard as a very estimable gentleman. But he has been most unfortunate in selecting his entourage." Nevertheless, he berated Tilden for committing himself so irrevocably to Green, regarded by Tammany as "gall and wormwood." [16] Cottman's analysis, used as a basis for action, was a self-fulfilling prophecy. The more frequently the influence of the ward leaders was taken as a reason for discrediting Kelly, the greater their influence became.

Kelly's paper, the New York *Express*, launched a bitter attack on the governor. Tilden, the paper charged in May, had ruined himself and the party by his overweening ambition to be President. The attack divided the city Democracy. At the caucus which preceded the opening of the Democratic National Convention in St. Louis, Kelly, August Belmont, Augustus Schell, former Congressman and Fenian leader William R. Roberts, and several Tammany officers all opposed Tilden's candidacy.[17] Kelly rose on the floor of the convention to urge the choice of a Western candidate. He promised that the delegates would regret the nomination of Tilden. Morrissey, who had been on friendly terms with the governor during the previous legislative session, swaggered through the corridors betting that Tilden would be nominated and elected. The first prediction proved correct and Kelly rose to affirm his loyalty to the party and to its candidate. Republican

[15] Sinnott to Tilden, New York, February 2, 1876, Tilden Papers.
[16] John Bigelow, ed., *Letters and Literary Memorials of Samuel J. Tilden* (New York: Harper, 1908), I, pp. 398–399.
[17] *Express*, May 10, 1876; *New York Tribune*, June 27, 1876.

policies, he charged, had encouraged unemployment, bankruptcy and the destruction of American commerce, "everything showing a tendency to destroy our businessmen." As a later New York meeting ratifying the nomination, Kelly promised that Tilden's victory would end the depression.[18] The ritual invocation of issues had begun.

The promise of loyalty did not still dissension. The underlying bitterness came to the surface at a Tammany Hall meeting on July 13. A delegate proposed an amendment to the resolutions of the Committee on Organization. The amendment expressed the General Committee's "unlimited confidence in the leadership of the Honorable John Kelly," and their assurance "that under that leadership the party in the coming contest will be conducted to victory." On Tilden's side, Peter Olney objected, and pandemonium broke loose. When quiet was restored, Edward Cooper vigorously attacked Kelly. Kelly, he charged, had represented Tammany opinion in St. Louis as antagonistic to Tilden quite without authorization. He condemned the *Express* for "vile slander."

The amendment was passed and Kelly entered the room. He attempted to assuage the ruffled tempers. "Perhaps it would have been better," he said when the shouting had died down, "if all this excitement had not taken place. The effect might be more injurious to the party than we are now willing to admit. There can be no difference in the issues that are now before the people or the candidates nominated at the St. Louis convention."

William Whitney made a similarly accommodating statement the following day. He dismissed plans to reorganize Tammany as figments of the journalistic imagination. Kelly, he contended, was a man of "too valuable influence, of too efficient control over certain elements of the party, to make it a matter of policy, to say nothing else, to dispense with his service." He had never heard any objections urged against Mr. Kelly "as a man." Edward Cooper was less sure that Kelly was a valuable figure. Cooper resented party discipline and he demanded "fuller representation

[18] *Official Proceedings of the National Democratic Convention, Held in St. Louis, Mo., June 27th, 28th, and 29, 1876* (St. Louis, 1876), p. 161; *New York Tribune,* July 15, 1876.

for thoughtful men." "Strong as Tammany is," he said, "it is not wholly representative, and it is thought by some not to allow sufficient latitude of action. There was a class of thoughful men within its halls that were not fully represented; then there is the German element and the Anti-Tammany Democracy. . . ." Cooper conceded that Kelly was a "legitimate" influence in the politics of the city, and so long as he remained useful there could be "no disposition to have him removed." He suggested, however, that special clubs be established for the campaign which would be more "representative." Though he was skeptical that Kelly would accept such a role, Tammany, he argued, would do well to confine its activities to the local election.[19]

A grudging unity developed in Democratic ranks for the national campaign, though Tilden did not trust Kelly's good faith or his ability to bring out the Irish vote. Former Governor Horatio Seymour warned Tilden that "reform" was not really a popular word with workingmen. The Republicans, hoping to gain strength in the cities, had dropped their attack on the creeping Catholic menace to the public schools. "I think it important," Seymour told Tilden, "that some quiet, judicious person should visit the large towns and see the leading Irishmen and call their minds back to the hostility of Hayes and the Republicans to their nationality and religion.[20] Seymour wanted to berate the Irish and eat them too.

Tilden carried the city handily. His plurality was larger than it had been in 1874 and nearly equalled Seymour's in the suspect election of 1868. The Democratic local ticket was also successful. Smith Ely, Jr., leather merchant and former Congressmen whom Tammany had nominated for mayor, defeated his Republican opponent, John Dix, by a vote of nearly two to one. John Robinson, Democratic candidate for governor, won the city with almost equal ease.

Morrissey's St. Louis bets on the election had to be cancelled. After several months of bitter dispute and prolonged negotiation, Rutherford Hayes and not Tilden was "elected" President. The

[19] *New York Tribune,* July 15, 1876.
[20] John Bigelow, ed., *Letters and Literary Memorials of Samuel J. Tilden* (New York: Harper, 1908), I, p. 470.

vote which Tammany had brought out, or could claim to have brought out, coupled with Tilden's defeat, seemed to leave Kelly in firm control of the city party. Green's term as comptroller expired in December and after some delay, Wickham appointed Kelly to the vacant office.

Tammany's electoral success did not obscure the fact that Tilden had encouraged the enemies of Kelly's power. The Governor had not formed a class party against the Tammany directorate but an anti-authority coalition which suited men with very different incomes, backgrounds, and styles.

Communication between previously separate groups often emerges as they are joined in a common battle against a centralizing power. This is what happened in New York in the 1870's. In the terms of the abstract model presented in Chapter One, lines appear along the periphery of the organization. Political coalitions based solely on a common enemy are, however, inherently unstable. Leaders of such a coalition, after they have succeeded in overthrowing the initial foe, may conjure up external threats to help achieve social unity and political stability. In most cases, however, the coalition divides and the political system, only a little altered, returns to its previous state.

The most important glimmer of change in American cities stemming from the repeated battles of the periphery against the center was a growing realization on the part of some of the dissidents that communication and cooperation among diverse groups was absolutely essential. By the twentieth century, many of Tilden's apparent political descendants had gained a new respect for the virtues of the centralized political machine. In the mid-1870's, however, Tilden's allies were both scornful and afraid. The depths of their antagonism to central direction is apparent when we compare the reform picture of Kelly with the Boss's behavior. Far from insisting on the new possibilities of political leadership, Kelly made every attempt to convince the city that he was the very model of a reform politician, committed to economy and limited government. Despite his protestations, he appeared—or so the reformers said—to be a despot.

THIRTEEN

The Growth of Regulation

The impact of the reform movement and the depression of the seventies was to increase the pressure for the decentralization of power and reliance upon the market for the distribution of income. Broad proposals for public promotion or development of the physical environment of the city were drastically curtailed or erratically pursued.

Beneath this gross pattern of decentralization and reliance on the market, New York was subtly changing. The dynamics of this change may be new to those who assume that government regulation is always opposed by businessmen. Many New York businessmen and professionals asked for the limitation of public planning and development in the city, and at the same time called upon the state to expand the flow of information between firms and to coordinate their activities through regulation. The use of the state as an instrument of business coordination reflected a rough calculation that the costs of control were lower than the mounting costs of competition.

Financial institutions, to use a concrete example of the growth of regulation in the middle and late seventies, were specially singled out for governmental control. The general public, it is true, had a strong interest in their security. The actual course of regulation, however, was decisively shaped by the special interests of firms within the financial community. The political instruments of the city and state were extremely sensitive to special and concerted demands. Diffuse general needs and demands, paradoxically, had few representatives.

The political experiences of the various sectors of the financial community were not precisely the same. Fire and life underwriters, for example, were both regulated by state law and reported to the superintendent of the insurance department. Control in the one case was a matter of constant contention and recrimination and in the other it was not. The differences stemmed from variations in the structures of the competing firms and of the industries in which they operated.

Most of the fire insurance companies were joint stock enterprises with a limited number of shareholders. The responsibility of their officers was clearly defined. The life insurance companies, in contrast, anticipated the structure of the giant twentieth century business corporation. The rights of ownership and management, even in the proprietary companies, were effectively separated. The officers enjoyed essentially irresponsible power. The policyholders, therefore, were forced to use the institutional mechanisms of the state, rather than the company, to protect their "rights." The state mechanism was relatively open, responsive, and familiar to them. The major "policyholders' revolt" of the decade placed pressure upon a company by arousing the legislature, and not by waiting for a corporate election. The Mutual in 1878 offered a large rebate on the first premiums of new contracts. The old policyholders complained bitterly that they were being discriminated against unfairly. Other companies charged that the Mutual was cutting rates below the point of safety. A legislative investigation ensued and the Mutual backed down in favor of a general reduction of premiums.[1]

Stockholders could not organize well enough to use the legislature to shape the policies of their companies in any detailed fashion. Politicians were encouraged to exploit, as much as to represent stockholders' complaints. The underwriters were probably correct. A good part of the regulatory measures introduced in Albany each year was "strike" legislation, intended only to force the companies to "buy off" the legislators.[2]

[1] Shepard B. Clough, *A Century of American Life Insurance, A History of the Mutual Life Insurance Company of New York, 1843–1943* (New York: Columbia University Press, 1946), pp. 141–144.
[2] James M. Hudnut, *Semi-Centennial History of the New York Life Insurance Company, 1845–1895* (New York: New York Life, 1895), p. 183; *New York Tribune*, March 6, 1874.

The life insurers were compelled to devote more of their energies to political activity than were the fire underwriters, because their policyholders used the state more than did those of the fire companies. The political efforts of the life insurers were usually successful. Policyholders asked the companies to establish an equity in their policies so that, in case a policyholder chose to leave a company, or failed to meet a premium payment, he would not lose everything he had already invested. Bills to force the companies to concede an equity value were introduced into almost every session of the legislature during the decade. One was successful, in 1879, only after many of the companies had already adopted contracts substantially granting what the law demanded. Companies were permitted to issue policies without equity provisions if they printed a waiver clause in red ink. New York Life began to print large sections of its policies in red.[3]

The political experiences of the life and fire insurance companies differed because of differences in the character of competition in the two branches of the industry. The life insurers faced the future with great certainty that men would die at a predictable rate. All the New York firms, after 1868, used an actuarial table developed by Sheppard Homans of Mutual Life, which required a 4½ percent reserve on all policies. The companies, working within the demands of Homans' tables, were forced to compete principally in the character of their policies, the strength of their reputations and the aggressiveness of their sales agents.

The fire insurance companies did not enjoy the same certainty, since they did not yet have a uniform table for the calculation of risks. They knew, moreover, that their own concerted action could reduce substantially the danger of calamitous fire. The history of the fire insurance firms was marked by attempts to set standard rates and to develop a uniform table of risks. The companies demanded that the city and state improve fire protection, provide adequate water and insist on safe building standards. The usual form of competition was price cutting.[4]

[3] R. Carlyle Buley, *The American Life Convention,* 1906–1925 (New York: Appleton-Century-Crofts, 1953), p. 100.
[4] Harry Chase Brearley, *Fifty Years of a Civilizing Force* (New York: Frederick A. Stokes, 1916), pp. 23–26, 36–41, 48–50, 57–59.

The non-price competition of the life insurers reinforced the pattern of political engagement. The principal contest in the industry was between the Mutual and the Equitable Life. The officers of the two companies, and those of other firms as they joined the lists, hired journalists to attack the reputations of their competitors, sued writers for defamation of character, traded insults and demanded investigations. Friends of the Mutual charged that the Chamber of Life Insurance, a trade association activated in 1873 to lobby for the industry, was a tool of the Equitable. The Equitable encouraged the complaints which forced the Mutual to back down on its rebates to new policyholders in 1878. The legislature conducted insurance investigations in 1873 and 1877. Both investigations originated in the recriminations of the officers of the two great rivals against one another and focused on the failings of the officers, rather than the more basic problems of the industry.[5]

The most important similarity in the political histories of the life and fire underwriters stemmed from the political efforts of well established firms to limit entry into their industry by setting standards for enterprise which only large companies could meet.

The insurance superintendent consistently urged the need for stricter control of new and unsafe firms. During most of the decade of the 1870's, New York law required that a fire insurance company doing business in New York or Brooklyn have an unimpaired and paid-up capital of $200,000. With the support of the established companies, the superintendent used his own discretion in restraining firms with a smaller capital from opening offices elsewhere in the state. He particularly prevented them from doing business on the borders of the prohibited counties. The legislature confirmed this administrative policy in 1877 and required the same minimum capital throughout the state.[6] Several small companies left the New York Board of Fire Underwriters in February, 1875. They charged that the board was run in the interest of large

---

[5] J. Owen Stalson, *Marketing Life Insurance* (Cambridge: Harvard University Press, 1942), pp. 422–427. The privately printed *Testimony Taken before the New York Assembly Committee on Insurance, 1877* (Albany, 1877), includes transcripts of both investigations.
[6] Superintendent of the Insurance Department of the State of New York, *Seventeenth Annual Report* (Albany, 1876) p. xx; *Nineteenth Annual Report* (Albany, 1878), p. xiii; *Laws, 1877*, c. 209.

American and foreign underwriters who set standards which new firms could not meet and which inhibited their attempt to attract business. The board, as if to prove the validity of the charge, proposed in 1878 that the legislature restrain companies from writing insurance beyond their net assets and increase the authority of the superintendent's office. The superintendent, for his part, bemoaned the collapse of the National Board of Fire Underwriters which had attempted to set uniform rates in the first half of the decade. He promised that he would refuse admission to speculative companies and would be very strict with any firm whose capital was impaired.[7] The life insurance companies raised $20,-000 in 1872 to increase the superintendent's prerogatives. Superintendent John Miller, in turn, boasted of his vigorous efforts to prosecute bogus companies with fictitious or insufficient capital.[8]

There were obvious limitations to a system of inspection directed principally to restricting entry. The superintendent did not, for example, have the authority to check management accounting procedures or to control the quality of investments. State regulation was impotent in the face of the massive failure of life insurance companies during the depression of 1873 to 1879. Only eight of the thirty-two firms chartered after 1861 remained in business in 1877. The large firms urged the superintendent at the beginning of the depression to carry along the imperiled companies. In the face of massive failures and general resentment, they became more insistent after 1876 that he refuse to tolerate any evasion of the law. They sponsored legislation to prevent companies on the verge of collapse from amalgamating with one another in the hope of avoiding inspection and sustaining their businesses.[9]

Insurance Superintendent John Smyth was caught in the middle of conflicting demands. Governor Robinson charged in 1877 that Smyth had allowed dangerously weak companies to go

[7] *New York Tribune,* February 8, 1875; August 8, 1877; Insurance Superintendent, *Nineteenth Annual Report,* pp. xxii-xxiii; *Testimony . . . on Insurance, 1877,* p. 32 b.
[8] Superintendent of the Insurance Department of New York, *Thirteenth Annual Report* (Albany, 1872), part 2, p. xxxi.
[9] *New York Tribune,* December 13, 16, 1876.

on writing insurance, had extorted excessive fees and had promoted political friends. The hearing, before the New York Senate, revealed both that Smyth was the victim of a politically motivated attack and, at the same time, that the charges were probably true. He admitted evading the regulations governing fees, but protested that he had done so only because the rules prevented him from conducting adequate inspections. The Senate refused to remove him and the Governor recommended that the insurance department be abandoned. Inspection had failed, he argued, and it would be better to do without it. Most insurance officers interviewed by the *Tribune* disagreed. They wished the department strengthened. Their chief complaint against state regulation was that it was too weak.[10] The complaint revealed a dimension in the history of government action in America which is missed by studies of regulation which focus exclusively on either the conflict between the business community and the public, or upon the activities of disinterested "reformers." Regulation was frequently a product of conflicts within the business community. The terms of conflict were shaped by the structure of economic markets and of the firms themselves.

The markets and types of firms in banking were more complex than in insurance. The difficulties of arriving at a settled basis of policy were, therefore, greater. The general pattern of regulation was, however, the same. Trust companies were placed under state supervision in 1874. Mortgage and safe deposit companies and savings banks were given uniform charters a year later. During the course of its passage through the legislature, the provision for actual inspection was removed from the general law for safe deposit companies. Banking Superintendent D. C. Ellis did not consider the omission crucial, but officers of several of the existing companies did. They urged strong supervision, rather than a delusive show of "publicity" figures. Under the proposed bill, they warned, unscrupulous men could establish an elaborate office for a new company, attract depositors and then abscond. Strong supervision and careful checking of applicants for charters would

---

[10] Charles Z. Lincoln, ed., *Messages from the Governors of the State of New York* (Albany: J. B. Lyon, 1909), VII, pp. 303–304; *Testimony Taken Before the Senate on Charges Against John F. Smyth, Superintendent of the Insurance Department* (Albany, 1878); *New York Tribune*, January 21, 1879.

prevent fraud in advance and limit the entry of new speculative firms. They urged Tilden to veto the "weak" bill.[11]

The large, well-established savings banks shared in drafting their general charter act. The officers of the Bowery Savings Bank, by far the largest savings institution in the city, commented with obvious gratification in 1876 that the "large interests confided to these savings banks demanded greater protection than was provided for in the special charters. The general law does not essentially differ from the original charter and the amendments granted to this institution." The secretary of a new Rochester bank, in contrast, wrote Tilden that the bill had "many objectionable features, particularly for young institutions who are working for an existence." [12]

The banking superintendent in 1876 pointed out that the 6 percent interest rate allowed in the general law benefited the older and larger banks. New and small banks, with few depositors and a small surplus could not afford 6 percent. To pay less than the old banks, he warned, is to discourage deposits; to pay the same is to prevent the accumulation of a safety fund. The new banks were established under "ill-advised legislation" but, he cautioned, they should not be driven to the wall by a high legal interest rate. He urged both a lowering of the maximum rate and the creation of a common safety fund to which all of the banks would contribute in order to insure against individual failures.[13] The larger banks successfully opposed the fund proposal. They accepted a lower interest rate in 1877, but protected their position carefully. The new law required a large individual bank reserve fund and a strict valuation of investments, again placing a heavy burden on the young banks.[14]

[11] D. C. Ellis to Tilden, Albany, June 8, 1875; Francis M. Jenks to Tilden, New York, June 3, 1875, Tilden Papers.

[12] Manual of the Bowery Savings Bank, Containing a History of the Institution, Original Charter, General Savings Bank Law, By-Laws, etc., etc. (New York, 1876), p. 43; P. B. Viele to Tilden, Rochester, April 17, 1875, Tilden Papers.

[13] Superintendent of the Banking Department, Annual Report Relative to Savings Banks, Transmitted to the Legislature, March 30, 1876 (Albany, 1876), pp. 20, 21.

[14] Superintendent of the Banking Department, Annual Report Relative to Savings Banks, Transmitted to the Legislature, May 6, 1877 (Albany, 1877), p. 16.

In the second half of the seventies, savings bank fell like a row of tipped dominoes. Seven New York banks failed in 1875, three more closed their doors in 1876, and seven in 1877-1878. The wave of failures, as in the insurance industry, left responsible state officials in the midst of conflicting interests. Superintendent Ellis was charged in the spring of 1877 with allowing banks to remain open after he knew that their investments had depreciated. Ellis protested that leading bankers had advised against precipitous action. He had only followed their advice. A Republican Senate saved Smyth; Ellis was removed as a sacrificial offering to "public opinion."[15]

Financial institutions were the only business firms significantly regulated by the government in the seventies. Debates over regulation were sometimes heated but, with a few exceptions which seemed increasingly old fashioned, conflicts over finance no longer generated the old ideological fervor of the days of Andrew Jackson. Private agreements among the banks and complex issues of administrative detail replaced the raging public discussion of the thirties and forties. The state had become, for most purposes, the instrument by which established firms expanded control over their industry and reduced the uncertainties of competition. The "railroad monster" took the place formerly occupied by the Monster Bank. Debates over railroad policy were still in the public domain. The faults of "railroad power" were a popular lecture theme and railroad reform was a plank in radical platforms. However, it was not this antagonism to the roads as a symbol which made the diabolical image and demand for social control politically significant, but the interest of businessmen in regulation.

Railroad executives, like their colleagues in banking and insurance, explored the possibilities of using the state as a coordinating agency. They did this because they were unhappy with private pooling agreements, setting rates and dividing markets, as instruments for sharing information and reducing competition. Individual lines were constantly tempted to try to "get away" with price cuts. Discovery led to retaliation and the abrogation of the agreement. To remedy this problem, several railroad officials in the late seventies began to argue for governmental regulation

[15] *New York Tribune*, May 17, August 2, 1877.

to allow for expanded supervision and mandatory compliance with price agreements.[16]

The railroad executives were opposed by New York shippers eager to break the pools rather than to strengthen them. This business opposition prevented the full articulation of the roads' argument. The presidents of the Central and Erie, shortly after signing a pooling agreement, were forced into the position of denouncing the "destructive communistic characteristics" of the Chamber of Commerce and associating the demand for regulation with a tendency to "socialistic principles" which threatened national disaster.[17]

The shippers, for their part, did not have special coercive powers of their own and they were dependent upon organization and public support for their success. The need to create and sustain the morale of their organization and to stir popular sentiment encouraged ideological appeals and a vivid imagery of the monster roads. Propaganda and ideology were rooted in organizational needs more than in initial systems of values.[18]

The merchants succeeded in obtaining a state legislative investigation of the railroads in 1879 because both parties were riddled with factional disputes. Contesting groups attempted to exploit a popular cause. Kelly apologized to the chairman of the Chamber of Commerce railroad committee in 1878 for not being able to convince the city's senators to vote for an investigating committee. New York politicians in 1879 could hardly be restrained from investigating the railroads.[19]

But investigating and acting were two very different matters. Despite the sweeping indictment prepared by the investigating committee under the guidance of Simon Sterne, the legislature, in the first years of the new decade, imposed only the most limited controls on the roads. Frustrated in their state efforts, the mer-

[16] Lee Benson, *Merchants, Farmers and Railroads, Railroad Regulation and New York Politics, 1850–1887* (Cambridge: Harvard University Press, 1955), pp. 233–234.
[17] Hepburn Committee, *Report of the Special Committee on Railroads . . . to Investigate Alleged Abuses in the Management of Railroads Chartered by the State of New York* (Albany, 1880), I, p. 70.
[18] Benson, *op. cit.*, describes the important role of New York merchants in the movement which led to the passage of the Interstate Commerce Act.
[19] This is the famous Hepburn Investigation (see footnote 17).

chants adopted an even more dramatically stated "anti-monopoly" stance and focused their attention on the development of national regulation. They failed in the state, essentially because the railroads, supported by many interior merchants and manufacturers, did not want the regulations which the New Yorkers demanded. In the case of the railroads, the insurance companies and banks, the leading firms probably got about as much regulation as they desired.

There was one other example in the seventies of a group of businessmen requesting regulation. The experiences of physicians and lawyers working to develop higher standards for entrance into their professions, were intriguingly similar to those of the "reform" savings banks and insurance companies.

The seventies were a turning point in the long trend toward greater democratization of the professions. The lawyers were more successful than the physicians in reversing the trend toward easy entry and uncontrolled competition. Their major weapons were strengthened state examining and licensing procedures. The principal backing for the new professional standards for lawyers came from the New York City Bar Association formed in 1870 to insist that the law was indeed a "noble profession," and not merely a "trade with the rest." [20] The association benefited from the cooperation of the institutional mechanism which stood directly athwart the point of entry—the courts.

The energies of the new association were devoted to raising the requirements for admission to the bar and to "purifying" the judiciary. The legislature authorized the Court of Appeals in 1871 to establish new rules regulating admission. The court reinstituted a period of clerkship, but exempted law school graduates from this practical apprenticeship and from public examinations. Untrained lawyers poured through this breach in the walls of the profession. A committee of the association, in January, 1876, demanded that the law schools require two years of study of all degree candidates, and that graduates spend one year as clerks in a lawyer's office before entering the bar. If the schools failed to reform, the committee insisted, they should lose all of their privileges. Prospective

[20] *Albany Law Journal,* I (March 12, 1870), pp. 203–204.

lawyers who were not college graduates, the committee suggested, should spend seven years as clerks. A permanent testing board should be established and written examinations required of all candidates.[21]

New regulations confirmed by the Court of Appeals in April, 1876, were less demanding than those requested by the Bar Association, but they marked a substantial step towards a new professional character for the practice of law. The *Albany Law Journal* expressed its satisfaction with the new regulations. The profession, the *Journal* hoped, would be characterized in the future by a new exclusiveness, greater competency and honesty.[22]

Attempts were also made in the seventies to strengthen professional standards regulating the practice of medicine. The New York Medico-Legal Society, formed to deal with the legal problems of the profession, prepared a bill in 1872 which authorized county medical societies to license all physicians, and to control the practice of medicine in their districts. The state would invest the profession itself with legal powers of regulation. The bill engendered substantial opposition. It placed authority in the hands of societies dominated by allopathic physicians, committed by the American Medical Association's Code of Ethical Practice, to avoid all professional contact with homeopathic doctors.[23] A circular was distributed throughout the state arousing all homeopaths, "advertising physicians," patent medicine proprietors, and "druggists doing a counter business," to oppose the "iniquitous" measure. The State Medical Society itself refused to endorse the bill. Some members of the society looked upon state regulation of any kind with suspicion and some of the local organizations in upstate counties included homeopaths. The bill passed the legislature only to be vetoed by Governor Hoffman. Public desires in the market place, Hoffman argued, were the only possible regulators

[21] *Albany Law Journal,* XVI (January 29, 1876), pp. 67–68.
[22] *Albany Law Journal,* XVI (October 6, 1877), pp. 229, 242.
[23] This distinction, introduced by Dr. Samuel Hahnemann, has largely vanished. Hahnemann used homeopathic drugs which produced effects similar to those of which the patient complained. Allopaths chose drugs producing a different effect. In practice, allopathy came to refer to the general practice of medicine without special regard for any particular form of treatment.

of medical practice. "So long as people are willing to employ irregular practitioners, so long will candidates for their patronage present themselves. No penal legislation will stop this, nor will this bill, if it becomes a law, remain for many years." [24]

Further efforts were made to pass the Medico-Legal Society bill in 1873 and 1874, but without success. A compromise measure was approved in 1874. The county societies were authorized to test and license all physicians who were not graduates of medical schools. The administrative procedures established by the act were so obviously clumsy, and the law so riddled with exceptions, that it was immediately denounced as a travesty of the original bill.[25] A good part of the politics of the medical profession during the next fifteen years revolved around attempts to clarify and mitigate the confusions engendered by the 1874 law.

Many physicians in the seventies began to argue that direct state licensing, rather than certification by either the schools or the societies, would be the most effective means of instituting professional controls. The New York Academy of Medicine consistently advocated this view. The President of the State Medical Society endorsed exclusive state licensing in 1879. Only small steps were actually taken in this direction. The state regents were empowered in 1872 to license physicians who presented themselves for examination.[26]

Physicians, at the end of the seventies, were understandably less pleased with their success in setting professional standards than were lawyers. Quackery was perhaps more dangerous in medicine than in law, but the adversary system and the courts' insistence on proper forms tended to discourage legal mistakes more readily than patients' complaints and Death's silence censured the errors of a physician. The best efforts of physicians did not always yield success—quackery was not easy to define! The codes of the New York Medical Society and the American Medical

---

[24] *New York Medical Journal,* XV (March, 1872), p. 327; XVII (March, 1873), p. 307; Lincoln, ed., *Messages of the Governors,* VI, p. 516.
[25] *New York Medical Journal,* XX (July, 1874), pp. 64–72; *Laws, 1874,* c. 436.
[26] James J. Walsh, *History of Medicine in New York* (New York: National Americana Society, 1919), I, pp. 83–87, 682; *New York Tribune,* February 6, 1879.

Association lumped all "irregular" physicians together, but many allopaths were not so rigid. They consulted and cooperated with homeopaths and did not consider them frauds. The State Medical Society, in 1882, attempted to abandon the A.M.A. and was expelled from the national organization. The legislature, as the historian of New York medicine notes, might have cooperated more fully in setting high standards if the profession had agreed on what the standards should be.[27]

This comment about medical practice captures the essential character of the drive towards public control or coordination of business enterprise during the 1870's. The state acted when an industry was structured so that its members, or some very strong group of its members, realized the intimate relationship between their own activities. They were able to watch each other, rather than simply to rely on the list of prices current. From this perspective, they arrived at relatively stable points of agreement which could be cemented into legislation. In the absence of this agreement, Governor Hoffman's dictum ruled: the competitive market will out.

There was one major alternative—or at least complement—to oligopolistic regulation. In an address before the American Public Health Association in November, 1874, Dr. Stephen Smith offered a provocative explanation of the failure to set high medical standards.[28] In America, he argued, anyone may call himself a physician by merely posting a shingle on his door. "Before the law," he reported, "medicine occupied the position of the most ordinary handicraft, and is subjected to the same legal restrictions and obligations." Occasionally, laws have been passed which recognized the special status of the profession, but they lacked a "stable foundation in any appreciative and intelligent governing power." A mere breath of opposition led to their repeal. Physicians had understandably grown weary of fickle legislatures and now re-

---

[27] Walsh, op. cit., I, p. 143.
[28] Stephen Smith, "On the Reciprocal Relations of an Efficient Public Health Service and the Highest Educational Qualifications of the Medical Profession," Public Health, II, Reports and Papers Presented at the Meetings of the American Public Health Association in the Years 1874–1875 (New York, 1876), pp. 192–200.

sisted the idea of aid from the state. They prided themselves on the accomplishments of self-help and voluntary association. It was clear, at least to Smith, that the profession had failed in its efforts, and was doomed to failure if it did not enlist the resources of the state. The particular source of its failure lay in the medical schools. Where there is no legal standard, he contended, the schools tend to enlarge their profits by increasing the size of classes and the number of graduates. Only at great risk could physicians fall prey to their suspicion of politicians. "The only power which can give rank and character to medicine," he concluded, "is the state."

Smith described the prerequisites of effective regulation. It was not enough merely to pressure the legislature for a particular bill. The whole force of public sentiment was antagonistic to legislation in favor of a single business or profession. "The inalienable right of the individual to do or to be what he pleases asserts itself in the most imperious manners. Every man his own lawyer or his own doctor is an axiom which American education and custom ingrains in the citizens." A measure which opposed this sense could only be temporary. The public could not be cajoled out of its basic conviction by direct appeals. "There must be established in the public mind a fixed belief that their welfare requires the incorporation of certain new powers and functions into the civil administration," which would in the long run, he hoped, nurture the conviction that health was a public interest which could be best served by governmental regulation and the most demanding standards.

The physicians' dilemma, as Smith describe it, infected every other area of life in which government regulation was perceived as a possible balance weight, or complement, to permissive individualism. Effective regulation required the development of a broad public sentiment in favor of control, or at least the creation of a powerful elite which thought that regulation was in the public interest.

FOURTEEN

Administering a Complex Environment

In Boss Tweed's New York there was no specific and persistent public opinion of the sort Stephen Smith required. There was no single elite which could provide leadership in the manner he demanded. There were, instead, a series of elites that commanded the respect of many limited "publics." The fragmentation of power and respect curtailed the work of administrative agencies which attempted to regulate a complex environment in the general interest. In many areas of life, the agencies were only one of many contending pressure groups. Their rules were no more authoritative than any others. Bureaucrats, such as Stephen Smith, who attempted to develop a new conception of the public interest and governmental authority, confronted problems which stemmed both from these external limits on their effectiveness and from their own inadequacies. These dual and interacting limitations, are the subject of this chapter.

The business experiences of New Yorkers did not equip them to handle the complex problems of public administration. Governing a city required performing many functions upon many different "products." The characteristic nineteenth century firm performed only a single function upon a single product or line of products.[1] Business firms expanding their scope in the later decades of the century encountered many of the same problems which had earlier plagued the city. The benefits gained from the division of labor were dissipated by a breakdown of the administrative mechanism.

[1] Alfred D. Chandler, Jr., "The Beginnings of 'Big Business' in American Industry," *Business History Review*, XXXIII (Spring, 1959), pp. 4–6.

The flow of formal information did not expand rapidly enough to keep pace with the specialization of operations and the increase in the spatial distance between the parts of the firm.[2] The city, as reformers vouched (though not with great sympathy) faced all of these problems long before they engaged most businessmen. The efforts of city administrators with limited authority to attack a tangle of interconnected difficulties were, therefore, almost doomed to failure. Their morale suffered, and they tended to reject the formal objectives of their organizations as utopian. The policeman stopped enforcing the law, and the building inspector began to "go along" with the wishes of the builders.

New York businessmen showed considerable appreciation of the difficulties of public administration in areas which intimately affected them and were parallel to their own organizational problems. They readily grasped, for example, the sources of administrative inefficiency and corruption in the New York Customs House.

The mercantile community regarded customs officials in much the same way as the lower class looked upon the police. Merchants, the commissioner of customs sadly noted in 1874, have come to regard the customs service "rather as an agency of personal profit to those who obtained admission into it than as a part of the machinery of a popular government for collecting the revenue necessary to its support, and to look upon the customs officer rather as a parasite, unlawfully living upon themselves, than as a public servant in honorable service." The government seemed to the merchants "as alien in interest and hostile in feeling to themselves."[3]

A committee of the New York Chamber of Commerce reported on the need for customs reform in 1872. After a long list of specific suggestions, the committee concluded with a general analysis of the problems of change. Steamship lines had revolutionized shipping, and merchants had reorganized their firms to meet the new demands for speed and efficiency. Government agencies had

---

[2] Joseph A. Litterer, "Systematic Management: Design for Organizational Recoupling in American Manufacturing Firms," *Business History Review*, XXXVIII (Winter, 1963), pp. 369–391.

[3] Quoted by Leonard D. White, *The Republican Era, 1869–1901* (New York: Macmillan, 1958), p. 119.

been less responsive. Slowness in port and unnecessary detention, which might have been tolerated in more leisurely days, were now "fantastically expensive." The Customs House regulations filled more than ten volumes and only a few old experts could possibly know their way through the maze of regulations. "The business of buying merchandise abroad, of shipping it hither and paying upon it the lawful duties, or of shipping our own products to foreign parts," the committee concluded, "should be invested with no such intricacy that a person of average intelligence should be precluded from personally undertaking it." Reform in the revenue code, administrative practices, and the quality of the customs house personnel would save the necessity of "running the gauntlet of brokers and other experts, or needlessly taking up the time of officials who at present, in many instances, appear to have no clearer insight into the business at hand than the bewildered merchant himself."

Merchants, the committee insisted, had to take a good part of the responsibility for the slowness of reform. They had devoted more energy to changing the procedures of their own firms than to modernizing the Customs House.[4]

Adopting the committee's report, the Chamber of Commerce rejected a limiting amendment which attributed all the faults of the Customs House to political interference with its operations. Civil service reform, simplification of the revenue code, and administrative reorganization, they felt, would have to go hand in hand. A bad system, and not simply bad men, led to confusion, the selling of favors, and bribery at the gates of Manhattan.

It was more difficult to develop the administrative acumen necessary to solve the vastly more complex problems of the entire city. Confronted with problems which went far beyond anything undertaken by business management, political leaders frequently attempted to simplify their tasks by allowing private agencies to perform what were normally considered public functions. This was the characteristic response to the problems of the sick, the hungry, the orphaned, the aged, and the criminal. Private organizations took up the burdens of public administration. In 1867 the

[4] *Fourteenth Annual Report of the Chamber of Commerce of the State of New York for the Year 1871—'72* (New York, 1872), pp. 106–122.

legislature, to choose the most prominent example of the role of private organization, created a Board of State Commissioners of Public Charities to inspect all philanthropic institutions which received state aid. The board almost immediately requested an extension of its power to include all charities whether publically supported or not. Its powers were not extended until it was backed by the State Charities Aid Association. The Association, established in 1872 under the leadership of Louisa Lee Schuyler, who had served with distinction on the United States Sanitary Commission during the war, was created to "promote an active public interest in the New York State institutions of public charities, with a view to the physical, mental and moral improvement of their pauper inmates," and to "make the present pauper system more efficient and to bring such reforms in it as may be in accordance with the most enlightened views of Christianity, Science and Philanthropy." The president of the new association was Theodore Dwight, professor of law at Columbia and vice-president of the state board. A pattern of cooperation and interlocking interests was apparent at the very beginning.[5]

The legislature extended the board's power in 1873 to allow it to inspect every "charitable, eleemosynary, correctional or reformatory institution" in the state, with the exception of prisons. The commissioners were empowered to appoint a board of visitors in each county. The bill was drafted by Dorman Eaton, chairman of the Charities Aid Association's committee on legislation, with the understanding that the local units of the association would serve as the county boards. The arrangement by which public powers were mandated to a private organization in return for private financing of public activities lasted until 1880. A quarrel at the end of the seventies between the board and the association was resolved by the legislature in favor of the private organization. After the board broke off the visiting arrangement, the legislature quickly granted the association the right to inspect all county, city, and town almshouses.[6]

[5] *New York Tribune*, May 18, 1872.
[6] David M. Schneider and Albert Deutsch, *The History of Public Welfare in New York State, 1867–1940* (Chicago: University of Chicago Press, 1941), pp. 22–26.

The New York Society for the Prevention of Cruelty to Children received similar grants of public authority. The legislature in 1874 made parents of vagrant or mendicant children guilty of a misdemeanor. The society was founded in the following year to enforce the law. The society's first report clearly defined its purposes. Ample laws had been passed for the protection of little children, the society contended, but they were not enforced. The society proposed by "lawful means and with energy" to secure the prompt convictions and punishment of every parent who failed in his duty. Its agents were, in effect, privately paid policemen. The original charter of the society empowered it to search out offenders, bring complaints before magistrates, and secure police aid. These powers were later extended to include the direct right of arrest.[7]

Although charitable work could be assumed by a private agency no group of volunteers was willing to undertake the massive jobs of cleaning the streets or guarding the health of the city. After the abrogation of the private street cleaning contract in 1872, these tasks remained inescapably the city's own. Small concerned groups influenced the legislative definition of these tasks but could not ensure—they seemed, indeed, at times to inhibit—administrative fulfillment of their intentions. The legislature was responsive to the wishes of a concerted minority. The administrative agencies were less easily changed. In some sense, they were more democratic than the legislature in responding to the general apathy and desire to be free of restraint. There was a quality of ritual expiation in New York politics. The passage of a law testified to the city's good intentions. Administrative neglect allowed the relieved sinner to continue undisturbed.

The effectiveness of public action was inversely proportional to the number of necessary points of control. By far the most successful regulation in the public interest was the quarantine service.[8] Smuggling-in immigrants hardly paid, since entry was virtually free and unlimited. People therefore, would only pass

[7] New York Society for the Prevention of Cruelty to Children, *First Annual Report, 1876* (New York, 1876), pp. 6–7; *Laws, 1881,* c. 776.
[8] See the debate over the reformed service, *New York Tribune,* February 10 and April 12, 1876.

at one point. There was a real saving, however, in dumping garbage. Port officials told the Chamber of Commerce in 1874 that their powers were inadequate "to prevent daily depredations upon the waters of this harbor." Garbage was dumped from piers; steamers and tugboats dropped ashes over the side or through concealed pipes. Scows, supposed to dump the city's refuse far out to sea, saved time and money by discharging close to shore. New legislation drafted in 1875 by the Chamber of Commerce prohibited dumping cinders or ashes within the harbor and provided for city scows into which ships could dump their refuse. Conflicts of jurisdiction between the state and federal governments and the difficulties in attempting to enforce the law with a small staff contrived to frustrate the best of intentions. The waters and shores of New York remained strewn with debris.[9]

Houses presented even more difficult problems than the harbor. The stated goal of city policy was to promote safe, healthy homes in which families could enjoy a maximum of privacy. Agencies with broad powers but meagre funds could not fulfill this goal. Regulation alone, as Charles Loring Brace (friend of children) and the First International (friends of revolution) argued, was to begin with an inadequate policy. In an industry composed of many small builders and small owners, the reform assertion that "good houses could pay as well as shoddy ones," remained an unrealistic piety. Brace and the radicals argued in vain for public construction.[10]

The debate on public housing policy never involved serious consideration of any alternative other than private construction within the existing city plan and regulation of individual homes rather than neighborhoods. City officials occasionally attempted to shape rough zoning rules by inhibiting the construction of tenements in new areas. The inhibitions soon fell before the demands of real estate developers. The courts insisted that traditional restrictions on crowding were not applicable in New York. The state Supreme Court ruled in 1877 that the common law provision which invested property with a right to light and air, which it

[9] *New York Tribune*, September 14, 1878; *Twenty-first Annual Report of the Chamber of Commerce . . . 1878–'79* (New York, 1879), pp. 130–131, 139.
[10] Charles L. Brace, "Model Tenement Houses," *Plumber and Sanitary Engineer*, I (February, 1878), pp. 47–48; *Labor-Standard*, October 28, 1877.

had enjoyed for twenty years, did not apply. The right, the court argued, was purely "speculative." The common law of rural America and old England would stifle city growth.[11]

A limited attempt at zoning was made by the Board of Health in the early seventies. It tried to restrict slaughter houses to special areas, consolidating all slaughtering below 110th Street in two large abbatoirs. One abattoir was opened in 1875 but the board was forced to back down from its larger plans to eliminate all local slaughtering. "We were in advance of public opinion and capital," the president of the board admitted in 1878," "and the butchers finally would not sustain us."[12]

Without public development or neighborhood planning, housing regulation was confined to individual units. This was a massive task. The structural deficiencies of the houses and the closeness of the quarters created, and compounded, the habits of tenants unaccustomed to a crowded urban existence. Habits could not be changed as readily as physical structures. The best-intended improvements were frequently of no avail against the weight of custom.

The Board of Health and the Building Department won and cherished only a few precious victories. Wooden buildings were discouraged with the cooperation of the fire insurance companies. The dangers of epidemic disease were mitigated. The two agencies were forced basically to accept the defined limits of the existing system. The Board of Health, for example, defended the manufacturing of cigars in tenement houses. The board used conditions in the tobacco factories as a standard of judgment. Since home conditions were no worse than those in factories, the board refused to act against them.[13]

The two agencies regulating housing frequently boasted of public acceptance of their orders. The statistics they offered belied their claims. In May, June, and July of 1873 the Board of Health issued 5,386 orders and was forced to institute 759 suits for non-

[11] *Real Estate Record and Builders Guide*, XX (July 14, 1877), p. 555.

[12] *Public Health*, III, *Reports and Papers Presented at the Meetings of the American Public Health Association in the Year 1875–1876* (New York, 1877), pp. 24–31; *New York Tribune*, June 4, 1878.

[13] See the complaints of cigar workers, January 23, 1874, and reply by the Board of Health, January 27, 1874, Mayors Papers, Box 163.

compliance. The agencies faced the constant opposition of tenement house owners who treated them as representatives of a foreign power. The Taxpayers' Association of the Tenth, Eleventh, and Seventeenth Wards, for example, asked that the power of outside bureaucrats be curtailed. What New York needed, the association insisted, was "local self-government." [14]

The magnitude of the interrelated problems of the house and the tenant discouraged effective regulation. Salary reductions and petty exactions destroyed administrative morale. A scandal developed in the Building Department in 1877 which was characteristic of difficulties in other agencies. The head of the department, within the limits of a fixed budget, had managed to raise his own salary, while reducing the salaries of his inspectors. Men who a few years before had been earning $1800 annually were making $750 in 1876, and were subjected to periodic assessments on their meagre salaries. The inspectors were open to bribery, and violations of the building law were common. [15]

These administrative difficulties frustrated the reform hopes raised by the major Tenement House Law of 1879. Complex motives impelled men to desire housing regulation. The leader of the movement for regulation, Henry C. Meyer, was, however, very much like the bank and insurance reformers in his fundamental interests. Meyer was editor of the *Plumber and Sanitary Engineer*, and a large manufacturer of plumbing supplies. Through the pages of his journal, he denounced amateur and inept plumbing. He called for state licensing of plumbers and government inspection of plumbing in February, 1878. The Building Department, he insisted in March, should demand that all houses be properly fitted with sound fixtures. Speculative builders who raised capital on small margins to build shoddy houses should be driven out of business. Noting that savings banks and trust companies were unwilling to underwrite speculative building loans, he offered hope for the success of regulatory legislation. [16]

The *Plumber*, in December, 1878, sponsored a prize competi-

[14] "Petition and Memorial of the Taxpayers' Association of the Tenth, Eleventh and Seventeenth Wards of the City of New York," *New York Senate Documents*, 96th Session, 1873 (Albany, 1873), Vol. I, no. 23, pp. 1–3.
[15] *American Architect and Building News*, II (November 24, 1877), p. 373.
[16] Plumber and Sanitary Engineer, I (February and March, 1878), pp. 27, 62.

tion for tenement house designs on the standard 25 by 100 foot city lot. The walls of the winning design of a "dumbbell" tenement were shaped to allow a narrow air shaft in the middle of the building. The obviously unsatisfactory character of the design only demonstrated what the contest had intended to prove from the beginning. "It is impossible," the prize committee announced, "to secure the requirements of physical and moral health within these narrow and arbitrary limits." Only the most stringent regulations, the *Plumber* argued, would make the narrow city lot at all livable. "With the present license allowed to builders and landlords," the journal argued, "no capitalist with a conscience can attempt to compete with unscrupulous and sordid men, whose sole aim seems to be to crowd the largest number of persons under one roof at the highest rental." [17]

The prize competition was followed by a series of meetings, leading to the formation of the Sanitary Reform Society and the drafting of a bill for the control of tenements. The president of the society was James Gallatin, grandson of Jefferson's Secretary of the Treasury. Gallatin's father had been a leading New York banker. The board of directors included many of the wealthiest men in the city. The campaign to regulate tenements was neither a middle class movement nor a movement of reformers in any way outside of the main current of American life. The opposition to the bill was probably more genuinely middle class. Meyers, in 1884, estimated that the 20,000 tenements in the city were owned by 18,000 different men. [18]

The law which emerged from the legislature did not alter the standard city lot. It provided, however, that a tenement was to occupy no more than 65 percent of its lot. There were to be at least six hundred cubic feet of air space for each occupant, and each sleeping room was to have a window unless the Board of Health decided that adequate light and ventilation was otherwise provided. The board was empowered to require a landlord to place

---

[17] *Ibid.*, II (December, 1878, and March, 1879), pp. 2, 88, 90.
[18] James Gallitan, "Tenement House Reform in the City of New York," *Public Health*, VI, *Reports and Papers Presented at the Meetings of the American Public Health Association in the Year 1880* (Boston, 1881), pp. 309–317; Gordon Atkins, *Health, Housing and Poverty in New York City, 1865–1898* (Ann Arbor, 1947), p. 115.

a janitor in every building housing more than ten families. An annual fund of $10,000 was created to pay for no more than thirty housing inspectors.[19]

The provision for inspection was clearly inadequate in the face of the resistance of tenement owners. The building and housing industries were dominated by small speculative operators who not only could not afford to construct and maintain houses of the sort reformers demanded but who bore the heaviest burden of city taxes. They struggled to evade the law. The discretionary authority of the board was used freely to allow evasion. Investigators at the turn of the century found that many houses covered 85 or even 90 per cent of their lots. Fundamental changes in the character of housing for the poor, in the absence of government promotion, awaited changes in building technology, the structure of the building industry and the income of the tenants.[20]

The Sanitary Reform Society and its successor organizations almost inevitably shaped their policy on the basis of a limited knowledge of urban society. They tended, therefore, to hinge their hopes too narrowly upon physical reconstruction and supervision. They came to equate the sound house with the healthy city.[21] Contemporary conservatives may well ask what would have been the costs of a successful policy of regulation? Is it possible that the failure of public policy reflected a salutary correction to the unsound fiddlings of premature reformers? Does intensive industrialization require a government too ineffective to make humane decisions?

There are no easy answers to these questions. Society, usually unthinkingly, weighs allowing babies to grow sick and die against increasing the capital resources of industry. New York made its choice for industry in the seventies. Perhaps, dependent upon the market to allocate resources, it could make no other choice. In the

---

[19] *Laws, 1879*, c. 504.
[20] Robert W. De Forest and Lawrence Veiller, eds., *The Tenement House Problem* (New York: Macmillan, 1903), I, pp. 17–18; Edward C. Kirkland, *Industry Comes of Age, Business, Labor, and Public Policy, 1860–1897* (New York: Holt, Rinehart and Winston, 1961), pp. 259–261.
[21] Roy Lubove, *The Progressives and the Slums* (Pittsburgh: University of Pittsburgh Press, 1962), pp. 251–256.

long run, industry would be healthier if babies were well, but the city did not—could not—make the long term calculations and investments which would realize that happy state. For the moment, New York relied almost wholly upon the private aspirations of parents to safeguard the future.

The major costs of reform may have been not potential but real; not economic but political. These costs were most apparent in the battles over street cleaning. Every human and animal inhabitant of the city was a bearer of filth. The dirt and wastes did not sink to the bottom or move with the tides as they did in the harbor. They stayed where they had fallen. Cleaning the streets required enormous expenditures of manpower and money, and yet it was doomed to be inadequate. The combination of a large budget, a large work force and inevitable failure made street cleaning the subject of political controversy and partisan maneuvering.

In 1872 street cleaning was entrusted to a special bureau of the Police Department. The officers of the new bureau immediately expounded upon the difficulties of their task. In certain areas of the city, they argued as they began operations in June, no amount of cleaning would have the desired sanitary effect unless the Board of Health was able to force the owners or occupants of tenement houses "to keep them in a more tidy condition so far as relates to the temporary storage and final disposition of swill and garbage; and in many cases, of still more offensive and disease breeding matter." In July, the Superintendent complained that he could sweep until doom's day without success if the police did not enforce provisions against depositing garbage in the streets.[22]

The new bureau's failure to perform a miracle aroused a political storm in 1874. The Board of Aldermen and the legislature investigated the bureau. The unanimous conclusion of the legislative committee was that although the cost of street cleaning had almost doubled since the Tweed era, it was not at all certain that the work was better done. The police had completely failed to prevent garbage from being dumped into the streets. The bureau was infested with incompetent political employees. Supervisors were ignorant and disdainful of their duties and they levied assessments on their subordinates. The work force of the bureau, in its

[22] *New York Tribune,* June 10, July 2, 1872.

Street Cleaners, 1868: A large budget but inevitable failure. *Historical Pictures Service—Chicago*

turn, demanded contributions from householders. The committee recommended the creation of a separate board directly appointed by the governor.[23]

Mayor Havemeyer rejected these findings, but William Wickham, his successor, vowed a concerted drive to clean the streets. Administrative resolve at the highest level was not enough. Popular violation of the law and conflicting attempts to accommodate or alter these violations completely overcame the cleaners. In 1878, the Police Board attempted to solve its problems by adopting a system of block-by-block responsibility within the department.[24] This accounting system for guilt (very much like the Christian accounting attacked by the social gospelers of the next decade) had very little to do with the general sources of urban filth.

The new system did not take street cleaning out of politics. In anticipation of the 1878 election, Jackson Schultz pressed charges against the police commissioners for failing in their duty. The charges formed the basis for an attempt by Mayor Cooper to remove the Police Board in 1879. The report on street cleaning, prepared by Schultz and Thatcher M. Adams for the new Municipal Society (it stood for "public economy" and "able, faithful, public officers and agents"), is a characteristic critique of public administration in the decade of the 1870's. It carefully documented the steady reduction of expenditures on street cleaning from 1873 to 1877. Approximately $1,100,000 had been spent on cleaning in the first year; $725,000 in the last. The two men pointed out that the streets, even if the best claims of the bureau were accepted, were cleaned less frequently than those of London, Liverpool, Manchester, Boston, and Philadelphia. Apparatus was inadequate. Compliance with the law seemed futile. Even when garbage and ashes were separated by the householders, the police immediately recombined the two in a common cart. Delays in collection encouraged spilling refuse into the street.

Despite these problems, the basic reason that the bureau failed to satisfy the demand for clean streets, Schultz and Adams insisted, was "political influence." The bureau, they asserted, was managed "rather in the interest of party than of clean streets. . . .

[23] *New York Tribune*, April 11, 1874.
[24] *New York Tribune*, June 11, 1878.

From this wicked system of political patronage, this barter of office and employment for corrupt ends, grow all the evils of which we taxpayers have to complain." [25]

Schultz and Adams' analysis had important implications for future policy and future frustrations. There was no necessary reason for the welfare of the party and cleanliness of the streets to have been conflicting, rather than complementary, goals. The failure to clean the streets properly could not entirely be laid at the door of the politicians. It was, very likely, precisely because street cleaning under the conditions of the decade was doomed to failure that the cleaners lost faith in their own organization and took their prestige from an outside organization, the political party. The party, in turn, came to depend upon the patronage of the bureau and other governmental bodies like it. [26]

The extreme emphasis upon the responsibility of politicians and political influence for the failures of administrative agencies served only to antagonize the politicians, to obscure real problems, and to lead to false hopes. Indeed, the self-conscious reformers seemed consistently to generate their own frustration. At the end of the seventies they weakened the fragile political structure of the city. The depression encouraged businessmen and professionals to demand more coordination as a solution to their special problems. It made them, at the same time, increasingly hostile to the general expansion or consolidation of public power.

---

[25] Committee of the New York Municipal Society Appointed to Investigate the System of Street Cleaning as Administered by the Board of Police in the City of New York, *Report Read Before the Municipal Society, January 7th, 1878* (New York, 1878).

[26] There was a remarkable improvement in street cleaning at the end of the century under Colonel George E. Waring. Without firing the men whom he inherited from previous administrations, Charles Zuebelin reported, Waring "so altered their appearance that the bent and ragged crossing sweeper of the old days would not be recognized in the man in neat white duck suit, with military carriage. . . . They were the 'white wings' that never grew weary." *American Municipal Progress* (New York: Macmillan, 1916), pp. 75–76.

FIFTEEN

Giant Without Direction

The demand for economy engendered an attack on the very foundations of New York's political order. The Tilden Commission, reporting in March, 1877, proposed a series of constitutional amendments which would have reconstructed the city government and limited voting privileges.[1] The amendments assaulted the system which gave John Kelly his political strength at a time when he was desperately trying to prove his respectability, his devotion to economy, and his unwillingness to use the government to alter the distribution of income.

The members of the commission found municipalities throughout the state plagued by heavy debts and an excessive increase of annual expenditures for ordinary purposes. These heavy financial burdens did not seem to them, particularly in New York City, to have purchased any remarkable public benefits. The commission defined three principal reasons for the financial problems of urban centers. Governing boards were "incompetent and unfaithful." The introduction of state and national politics into municipal government disrupted administration and introduced irrelevent considerations into the choice of both policies and personnel. Cities, they contended, were business corporations and there was no reason for difference of principle or party to

[1] *Report of the Commission to Devise a Plan for the Government of Cities in the State of New York, Presented to the Legislature, March 6th, 1877* (New York, 1877). The report was signed by Evarts, Samuel Hand, E. L. Godkin, John A. Lott, Joshua M. Van Cott, James C. Carter, Oswald Ottendorfer, William Allen Butler, Simon Sterne and Henry D. Dimock. Hand disagreed with the proposal to form boards of finance elected by taxpayers.

enter into their affairs. Finally, the legislature had usurped control over local affairs. The legislators, in addition to being ignorant, felt no direct sense of responsibility for local concerns in areas other than their own.

The commission dismissed as ephemeral a whole list of solutions which, they insisted, treated only the symptoms and not the municipal disease. Penal laws to punish corrupt officials, while helpful, had to be enforced by public officers. The principal problems of the past had not been with the law but with enforcement. A statutory limit on borrowing would be evaded. It would not help to remove all power from local government (indeed legislative interference aggravated the difficulties of the cities) nor to centralize all authority in a single local executive officer. The commissioners challenged the idea that politics would be improved when the masses were enlightened. The presumption upon which a system of government must be founded, they argued, was that the citizenry would not in any large measure allocate its time or energies to public, rather than private, business. Governments are contrivances to protect the "industrious citizen" in his private pursuits. "When these contrivances . . . become themselves the occasion of incessant watchfulness and enormous expense they fail in their essential purposes. . . . Dedicated public-minded citizens engaged in reform works," they reported, "acknowledge the fruitlessness of any effort for improvement through the regular instrumentality of popular election."

Local government, the commission concluded, could be improved only if authority over expenditures was placed firmly in the hands of the interested taxpayers. The business of the state and national governments affected everyone. Muncipal government was the exclusive concern of those who paid for the limited services of the city. The commission proposed that municipalities throughout the state be given broad responsibility for local affairs, though the power to tax and incur debt should be limited by statute. Authority over revenues and expenditures should be vested in a Board of Finance, elected by those who paid taxes on property worth more than $5000 or a rent of $250 a year. This board should appoint the financial and legal officers of the city. Every local improvement should be approved by two thirds of the members of both the Board of Aldermen and the Board of

Finance. A majority of those assessed for a public project had to approve the measure in advance. Almost all public works not financed by assessments should be financed by direct taxation, and not by the issuance of bonds.

Successful constitutional amendments had to be approved by two successive sessions of the legislature, and ratified at a general election. The commission's proposals were immediately endorsed by every major New York business group.

Civil service reformer Dorman Eaton opened a public meeting supporting the amendments on April 7, 1877. The "right" and educated men of the city, he argued, neglected public affairs and left the government to be run by the "ignorant, the idle, the vicious and the scheming politicians. . . . The thieves, the gamblers, the grogshop politicians, all the partisan and supremely selfish interests," were combined against the amendments. Simon Sterne, following Eaton, dismissed the "preposterous" idea that "a mere majority should direct how the public expenses, paid by the minority, should be regulated."

William Evarts, chairman of the commission, defended its insistence on structural changes in the city government. The general interest, he argued, is not forwarded by popular movements or perpetual changes and experiments. "It is not by ferment, by noise, by its growth in popular movements that the popular will will be carried out. . . . It is by organization, which attaches to the popular will its time, its seasons, its methods of expression and of execution that shall accomplish that will and thus advance those interests of prosperity, of peace, of wealth and of growth." Great cities, he asserted, cannot stand, "that infinite progress even toward perfection that consists in annual changes and in monthly experiments." Approval of the amendments would allow the legislature to resume its old concern with measures to simplify commerce, promote industry, protect and advance liberty and education. The perpetual controversy "about the wages of aldermen, the salaries of office-holders and the methods by which offices are to be filled," would come to an end.[2]

The amendments were debated in the fall campaign. The Left's sense of an approaching cataclysm was more than matched in the taxpaying community. The city, a Municipal Society circular contended, is threatened by the decay of all business, insolvency, and lawlessness. Those who have property will run, and "those who have everything to gain by voting away the property of others will be supreme." The right of suffrage, the Society's circular argued, is not absolute but must be regulated "in reference to the public safety. . . . It was foolish to believe" that voting privileges which ruled in small towns and villages could be duplicated in large cities. "It might as well be declared," the circular went on, "that the simple open towns and villages, with their intelligent, orderly American population, have as many desperadoes from all ends of the earth, as many dark passages, low grog and junk-shops, houses of infamy and secret gambling dens, as many stores filled with rich silks and jewels, as many banks and safe-deposit vaults, filled with coin, greenbacks and bonds to be robbed, as vast a volume of stocks, notes, bills and letters of credit to be altered and forged, as many thousands of buidings to be protected from fire and robbery, as there are in the great cities. . . ." [3]

The businessmen demanding the constitutional amendments argued that effective city government depended upon the exclusion of a range of voters from political discussion. These voters were pictured as so dangerous that they could not be integrated into the community. Indeed, the city was not a political community at all. It was a business corporation. The fall of the Tweed Ring had discredited the tactics of social integration through giant payments to diverse groups. The amendments rejected the possibilities of unity through general enlightenment—through mass communications. Unity was, in reform eyes, an administrative problem, a problem of "good" government.

Kelly, of course, had to oppose the amendments. He did this with success but, in so doing he alienated reformers whom he was trying to appease. In the depths of the depression, labor and radical organizations urged the city to engage in an extensive program of public works and to avoid aiding the efforts of private employers to lower wages. First Wickham and then Ely and Kelly refused these urgings. They preached economy and a halt to municipal construction. Public outdoor relief was confined to the

[3] *New York Tribune,* November 1, 1877.

distribution of coal. The picket lines of strikers were broken and "loiterers" dispersed. Strikers, the police superintendent insisted, had no right even by their presence to intimidate anyone who wanted to work.[4]

Edward Cooper and several other of Tilden's friends left Tammany in 1877. Henry Clinton, chairman of the Tammany Hall General Committee, dismissed the defections. Tammany Hall, he claimed, was as strong as it had ever been, "in leadership, in discipline, in policy and in patronage." He complained, however, that its policy of economy was not justly appreciated. The city government, he contended, was run more efficiently under Kelly than under any comptroller in the preceding twenty years. There were no sinecures in the city government, "not a dozen in all the departments, and these few—if indeed there are any— have crept in through the appointments by judges of superfluous court officers." The General Committee had been increased to twelve hundred members to insure thorough canvassing of the city. Apart from a few carping critics, Clinton asserted, Kelly is "highly regarded among the best men in the community." [5] James Buell, president of the Importers and Traders National Bank, told a meeting of the American Bankers Association in September, that the finances of New York were in a more "hopeful" position than they had been in years.[6] In contrast, as the *Express* pointed out to the "respectables" who were joining forces against Tammany, Morrissey, their ally, was a pool seller, a "numbers king." [7]

Kelly successfully insisted at the State Democratic convention in September, that two of the major supporters of Tilden and Governor Robinson be dropped from the state ticket. The Anti-Tammany delegation to the state convention and several Tammany members, including Olney and Wickham, protested. Tilden, returning from Europe in the course of the campaign, warned that "any nominations that did not promise cooperation in the reform policy which I had the honor to inaugurate and which Governor

[4] *New York Tribune*, August 1, 1876.
[5] *New York Tribune*, August 3, 1877.
[6] American Bankers Association, *Reports of the Proceedings at Conventions of the American Bankers Association From Its Organization in 1875 to 1889* (New York, 1890), I, p. 95.
[7] *Express*, September 5, 1877.

Robinson is consummating will be disowned by the Democratic masses."[8]

The Anti-Tammany Democrats cooperated with the Republicans to nominate a local slate. The coalition was a curious one. Some of the Anti-Tammany leaders looked upon Morrissey as a traitor, others regarded him as a friend and an ally. The coalition was marked, as in the past, by differences in policy and by broad gaps between complaints and proposed solutions. The basic stability of city politics depended on these gaps. When the labor unions and socialists managed to mount a significant threat to the city parties in 1886, they chose as their candidate for Mayor, Henry George, who for all his single tax radicalism was skeptical about the role of labor unions in a free society and deeply antagonistic to socialism. On a smaller scale in 1877, speakers at one local meeting criticized Tammany for not distributing patronage in the district to labor union representatives, and then went on to request the political aid of Green and Ottendorfer.[9] Morrissey, the rough hewn gambler, had sponsored legislation to aid real estate owners in the previous session of the legislature. Running for state senator against Augustus Schell in the wealthy Murray Hill district, Morrisey boasted that he didn't see "how a man who owns property is going to vote against me, no matter what his politics are."[10]

The election was a decisive victory for Tammany. Victory did not, however, sweeten the relations between Kelly and Tilden. The Boss's political difficulties contrasted sharply with the praise heaped upon his policy by financiers. The comptroller played heavily upon the fact that debt had been reduced in 1877 for the first time in the decade. Green's budget for the year had been cut by $1,200,000, and the estimates for 1878 had been slashed another $900,000. A bill drafted by the comptroller to place the entire city debt, including assessment bonds, under one general sinking fund was introduced into the legislature early in 1878.[11]

The bill, coupled with the reduction of the debt, enhanced Kelly's reputation in the financial community. He was presented

[8] DeAlva Stanwood Alexander, *A Political History of the State of New York* (New York: Henry Hole, 1909), III, p. 385.
[9] *New York Tribune*, September 5, 1877.
[10] *New York Tribune*, November 3 ,1887.
[11] *New York Tribune*, November 9, 1877; January 11, 1878.

in April with a petition praising his "prompt, efficient and digni-
fied" management of the comptroller's office. The petitioners included seven of the eleven men to whom Green had addressed a
final justifying letter in 1876. The petition urged the comptroller
to work for a further reduction of expenditures so that the tax rate
might be cut to 2 percent. Kelly replied that he would press
assiduously for economy, but warned that valuable men who
could earn more in private business would be driven from the
public service by hasty reductions. He promised to work for good
government and to "ameliorate the heavy burdens of taxation
entailed upon our citizens by a wicked and corrupt administration
in the past." He was pleased to have the confidence of merchants
and bankers and pledged that their trust would not be misplaced.[12]

When the refunding bill was finally passed after a full measure
of political back-biting, the dreams of grandeur which had possessed New York in the sixties were effectively limited. A new
redemption fund was established. It was to be sustained by income
from assessments and from increased taxes levied with each new
bond issue. Deficits in the fund would be met by a required yearly
appropriation of between one and two million dollars. A policy
of "fiscal responsibility" and at least partial "pay as you go" taxation inhibited large-scale advance planning for future growth.

Kelly boasted of his commitment to economy. At the beginning of the decade Havemeyer had opposed the Brooklyn Bridge
and Kelly had championed the project. He reversed his field in
1878. The bridge had been a totally public project since 1875,
when the legislature had bailed out the private companies engaged
in the construction of the great span. New York and Brooklyn
were authorized to allocate $8,000,000 to complete the project.
When the bridge authorities asked New York for its share in 1878,
Kelly supported the bitterly antagonistic Council of Political Reform. Any money spent on the bridge, he argued, would be
wasted. As a citizen and as a taxpayer he was opposed to further
appropriations. The bridge would be inadequate and all the
benefits would go to Brooklyn.[13]

[12] *New York Tribune*, March 29, 1878. Compare with Green's letter, *New York Tribune*, December 8, 1876.
[13] *New York Tribune*, August 14, 1878.

Kelly struck the classic posture of reform in a second area. Almost from the first moment of his appointment, Tammany had been conducting a running battle with Allan Campbell, the Public Works Commissioner who had replaced Fitz John Porter. Campbell denied patronage to Tammany and lent his support to Anti-Tammany Democrats. The battle reached a new intensity in 1878. Campbell contended that at least 50 of the 300 miles of paved streets in the city were impassable. They consisted of rotten wooden pavements, dilapidated cobblestones, and eroded stone blocks. The city, moreover, did not have sufficient carrying and pumping capacity to deliver water to houses on high ground. He had pleaded in vain for appropriations. The law of 1875 allowed New York to spend up to $500,000 a year for repavement, but his requests had been systematically denied or ruthlessly cut. The Board of Estimate and Apportionment had allocated a total of $500,000 for the three years, 1876, 1877, and 1878, since the passage of the law. Campbell had wanted to try an asphalt block pavement but Kelly had opposed the experiment. The courts had interpreted an 1875 act as prohibiting repavement at private expense even when the owners were willing to undertake the costs of improvement. Campbell complained that he had been unable to convince the legislature to amend the law.[14]

Kelly, conjuring up a distorted image of Green's rhetoric, charged that Campbell was a poor administrator. Projects under his direction had been inefficiently and shoddily done at an excessive cost. Economies in the Public Works Department, such as they were, were the result of the efforts of the Board of Estimate and not the commissioner. Reversing field neatly, Kelly charged that Campbell had executed by day-labor projects which would have been better let by contract.[15]

Kelly played the part of municipal economizer in one final area. Early in 1877 he had warned that municipal salaries could be lowered only at the risk of the wholesale disruption of public services. Supervisory personnel in most departments were paid less than they would have received in private firms and the city was already burdened by hidden costs from the meanness of its

[14] *New York Tribune,* February 19, August 20, September 12, 1878.
[15] *New York Tribune,* August 8, September 13, 1878.

salaries. Further reductions would have increased the illicit sale of city services and extortion from subordinates. A few city posts, notably those supported by fees, were very remunerative and by contemporary standards the officeholders were overpaid. Kelly was ready, therefore, to abandon the system of fees and to introduce a fixed salary scale. He was struggling to break with the tradition of the cash pay-off as the major instrument of party coordination and was willing to concede that the city government could not be organized as an entrepreneurial venture.[16] In 1878 he supported a bill to place the coroners on a salary. Under the pressure of the demand for economy, he went even further. He urged the legislature to allow the Board of Estimate and Apportionment to reduce general salaries so that the 1879 tax levy would be $2,000,000 less than it had been in 1878. Governor Robinson vetoed the reduction bill, arguing that it gave the Board of Estimate "despotic powers." [17]

The culmination of Kelly's claim to acceptance by the business community came at a meeting of "independent" businessmen at the beginning of October, 1878. The conferees were interested in nominating a mayor dedicated to lowering the tax rate to 2 per cent. Charles Fry of the Bank of New York presided over the meeting, which included many of the bankers and insurance executives who approval Kelly avidly sought.

The meeting proposed the names of five men as possible candidates for mayor and Kelly said that any of them would be excellent.[18] Two days after the meeting, a syndicate of Drexel, Morgan and Company, August Belmont and Company, and Winslow, Lanier and Company offered to purchase an entire issue of $6,900,000 of city 5 percent bonds at a premium of $5.28 on each $100. This was the highest premium offered by an underwriter during the entire decade.[19] This rise in the premium on city bonds poses an interesting question: was economy necessary? The evidence is conflicting. Early in 1877, Chamberlain George

[16] New York Tribune, April 3, 1878.
[17] Charles Z. Lincoln, ed., Messages from the Governors of the State of New York (Albany: J. B. Lyon, 1000), VII, p. 252–257.
[18] Express, October 7, 1878.
[19] New York Tribune, October 9, 1878.

W. Lane, the formal custodian of the city treasury, reported that financial institutions felt that New York securities would not be safe investments if the debt continued to rise. If expenses were not cut they would dispose of their holdings and refuse to purchase any further issues.[20]

There is some independent data supporting Lane's contention. Frederick Winston, president of the Mutual Life Insurance Company, reported to his trustees in July, 1876, that the city debt amounted to about $106 per person and 7½ cents on each dollar of assessed real and personal property. The company's present holdings were safe. He wondered, however, whether it would not be wise to restrict further purchases of New York bonds, and to place some limit on investment in city real estate. New York, he contended, was losing its predominance to inland cities. Its commercial facilities were inadequate and its laborers were likely to live outside the city limits even after the construction of the els.[21]

The financial evidence was not all one-sided. Ex-mayor Wickham, questioning Lane's apprehensions, noted that even in 1877 city bonds sold at a premium and were among the best securities on the market.[22] Through the rest of the decade, bankers bid eagerly for municipal debentures. It is by no means clear that the limits of the ability of the local government to mitigate the depression had been reached. A counter-cyclical policy was apparently blocked by the general apprehensions of businessmen and taxpayers rather than by the specific reluctance of investors to purchase city bonds. A policy of new public works and increased welfare expenditures, including low cost housing, might have yielded direct immediate benefits and would have had a multiplier effect upon employment. At any rate, the city's policies of reducing the debt and cutting expenditures probably aggravated the depression.[23]

There was something touching about Kelly's economy and

[20] *New York Tribune,* January 24, 1877.
[21] F. S. Winston, President of the Mutual Life Insurance Company, *Facts and Observations as to Financial and Business Affairs Generally* . . . *July, 1876* (New York, 1876), pp. 3–6.
[22] *New York Tribune,* January 24, 1877.
[23] The possibilities and limits of local fiscal policy are discussed by Alvin H. Hansen and Harvey S. Perloff, *State and Local Finance in the National Economy* (New York: W. W. Norton, 1944), pp. 194–200.

reform stance. The comptroller, Henry Clinton asserted, is as "pure as the sun." [24] How Tweed would have smiled at the image. The old boss died in prison on April 12, 1878. He had suffered through a stormy seven years. In and out of jail—once in an exciting backdoor escape and flight to Spain—he must have wondered at the transformation of his party and his city. To the question: "Could honest men act as effectively as thieves?" he probably would have answered a resounding, "No!"

They could not, it would seem, even win elections quite as well. Clinton's boast of Kelly's purity expressed a desperate but futile desire for acceptance. The desire was not fulfilled. The deep irony of the reform attack on Kelly was its association with demands for new public improvements. Tammany's opponents urged a reduction of taxes and, at the same time, public projects to improve the city and to provide employment. "Our only aims," said Thomas Cooper Campbell, the son of the Public Works Commissioner, "are a good police force, good pavements, substantial docks, a well-lighted and a healthy city, a good fire department, economic expenditure and honest and efficient administration." [25] Tammany Hall was charged with the defeat of bills for needed public improvements. Morrissey's old friends were particularly insistent that any party which did not get on the "wave of protest against capital," would lose the next election. The business of government, Ira Shafer, one of the old-line Anti-Tammany politicians, contended, is aid to the workingman. The meeting at which he spoke went on to endorse Tilden and Robinson.[26]

The endorsement mocked Shafer's statement of principles. Some Anti-Tammany politicians recognized the irony. They were particularly apprehensive that the victory of their mayoralty candidate, Edward Cooper, would bring Green back to office. They requested, and may have received, a promise from Cooper not to reappoint the former comptroller. Fundamentally, however, the political system operated as if men believed that radical purposes would be served by an opportunistic policy which stayed within the existing political framework.

Cooper's supporters made Kelly's leadership the major issue

[24] *New York Tribune*, September 1, 1878.
[25] *New York Tribune*, September 12, 1878.
[26] *New York Tribune*, October 7, 10, 1878.

of their campaign. Their attacks were not directed against the man but against his system. "The fact is," charged Abram Hewitt, who was denied the Tammany nomination for Congress, "John Kelly has become as absolute a dictator as was known in the history of Rome; and if his power is not broken in the coming election, it is impossible to say where it will end." Hewitt conceded that Kelly was both "pure and honest." "I have no doubt," he went on, "that he thinks he is performing a patriotic duty and wielding his vast power for the public good; but he is not a man of sufficient breadth of intellect to realize the results of the political system which he is establishing when carried to their logical conclusions." Kelly's leadership, Hewitt concluded, "is by no means an unmixed evil, but the results of such absolute leadership must in the end be disastrous to free government." [27] A committee of the Municipal Society, endorsing Cooper, conceded that "under John Kelly's management Tammany Hall is not a corrupt organization except as such an organization must be corrupt in making spoils of office, and as the domination of a single head is necessarily opposed to the American idea." [28]

As the election returns indicating Cooper's victory poured in, the epitaph for Kelly's reform aspirations was read by an unnamed partisan of Tammany Hall. "Well you see," he said, explaining the defeat, "times are hard and the workingmen need work. We have not given them any. The other side promised them some. And then, our reduction of the expenses of government hasn't been popular with the laboring classes, and besides, we have had the folly to boast of our reductions." [29]

Cooper proclaimed an end to the "niggardly policy" of previous administrations. City development under public auspices was, however, never again in the nineteenth century infused with the same impetus, the same vaulting ambition, that it had enjoyed in the first post-Civil War years. The opportunity to anticipate the needs of the population and to restructure the physical environment of the city had been lost. It would take enormous efforts to catch up and stabilize the new and untamed urban frontier. The

[27] *New York Tribune*, October 25, 1878.
[28] *New York Tribune*, October 25, 1878.
[29] *New York Tribune*, November 6, 1878.

hesitancy about power which infected the development program touched the party structure. Kelly walked out of the Democratic State Convention, and the Anti-Tammany Party supplanted Tammany as the "regular" organization in the city. Cooper was unable to build a stable coalition and the city marked political time in the first half of the eighties as rival factions battled. Having condemned Tammany for its overweening power, the reformers were unable to construct a new and stable institution in its place. An unstable political structure—a divided society—accommodated rapid change but could not control it. New York was, better than the Municipal Society knew, a city committed to the "American idea," a city—a giant—without direction.

SIXTEEN

Communication and Social Change

This book pictures New York in two complementary ways. First, the city is painted as a giant metropolis connected to the larger world around it by a complex transportation and communications network. The second view, turning in on the city itself, sees it as a fragmented mass, only loosely held together by its internal street car lines, newspapers, mail routes and associations.

I have only briefly treated the elements of the larger picture, though they were obviously of profound importance. A good deal of the argument which has been applied to internal urban change is also applicable to the national and international sphere. The city did not gain a profound understanding of conditions in Alabama, in Kansas, or in Havana from its limited channels of communication. Policy towards the South, for example, was dictated by the short-run desire of investors for stability and by a profound conviction that it was impossible to manipulate a distant environment. Agrarian problems were viewed through a series of limiting stereotypes as narrow as those with which the Western and Southern radicals imagined the metropolis. New York's few attempts to impose a national policy upon the diverse nation—attempts dictated by immediate economic self-interest—usually managed to accentuate the market distribution of income and to inhibit the growth of other sections.

Within New York, the narrow lines of communication between men and their limited ability to deal with complex information fragmented society. The men who made important decisions were forced to simplify complex problems. Decentralized decision-making was embedded in both the values and the practice of the city. The most common form of decentralization—and simplification—was reliance upon the free operations of the market place. Tweed's purchases of political support and his thievery were simply the ultimate extension of the dominance of the dollar-vote. Centralization or coordination intended to limit reliance upon the market loomed in the minds of New York's isolated citizens as illegitimate autocracy.

These two pictures of the city are dynamic and inter-related. In the largest sense, as C. Vann Woodward has argued,[1] the fragmentation of nineteenth century society was encouraged by the great peace of the Western world. The United States enjoyed security without paying for it and without having to organize its energies in its own defense. The demise of free security in the twentieth century has been a powerful force impelling domestic social cohesion. In smaller ways, problems in New York's external relationships in the 1860's and 1870's led to the formation of city groups able to operate for the first time in effective organizations. Merchants, for example, came together to reduce railroad rates.

Change within the city also generated increased demands for improved communication. As men grew closer together the costs of the failure to share information, to distinguish and to analyze the elements of a complex world, grew more and more costly. Businessmen were increasingly unhappy with their inability to control the operations of their firms and the fluctuations of the market. Laborers protested against their inability to communicate effectively with their bosses. Churchmen worried that they had lost contact with the urban poor. The costs of decentralized planning and administration in the expanding cities multiplied. The moral and epistemoligical tactics which limited the search for information creaked under the weight of unresolved problems.

Proof that new investments in communication and knowledge were precipitated by changes in the values and costs of information remains, in this book, highly impressionistic. I have relied upon the testimony of contemporaries: the moanings of charity workers at the social costs of their ignorance, the complaints of bankers and physicians about "hidden" competition, the fears

[1] C. Van Woodward, "The Age of Reinterpretation," *American Historical Review*, LXVI (1960), 1–19.

of ministers and insurance executives that they were "out of touch." A more objective measurement of the worth and cost of knowledge would test the argument, allow comparative investigation of different cities and different societies, and give us some sense of whether obvious improvements in communication and information systems had kept pace with the rising costs of ignorance and uncertainty.

The fact of improvement in communication and in the ability to analyze complex information is one of the most striking characteristics of the American experience since 1870. In the few decades after Tweed's death a vast world of mass communication was explored in all its sensationalist depths. Businessmen developed new means of sharing information and coordinating their activities. The voluminous flow of limited price messages between many small competitive units was largely replaced in many areas by a simplified external market network and a complex flow of information within individual firms. Ministers linked their churches together in order to "reach" the lower classes. Social workers established centers to connect the inhabitants of poor neighborhoods with each other and with the outside world. Educational reformers argued that the teacher could not communicate, could not create a democratic community, unless he attempted to discover his students. Social scientists insisted that they could only make sense of a world of anomalous information if they adopted a pragmatic rather than an absolutist epistemology.

Living as we do in an age of great bureaucratic organizations we are frequently, and properly, concerned with preserving individual spontaneity and freedom against the weight of institutional coordinators. The decentralized market society of the nineteenth century may tempt us as an answer to our contemporary dilemmas. Nostalgia should not obscure our vision. Decentralization enthroned both the sovereign individual and thousands of local autocrats. Reliance on the market narrowed the range of important social information to a few simple elements: "How much will you supply?" and "How much will you pay?"

Surely, even if each man had his price, there was more to a human being than an attached dollar sign. The expansion of the communications network in the late nineteenth and twentieth centuries, the attack on local autocrats and local majorities, and the demands for more complex information opened new opportunities for freedom and creativity. The radical vision of a society united by a rich flow of communication and fostering individual spontaneity must be brought to bear against both the world of the nineteenth century and the use of the new technical and institutional media to inhibit and coerce the human spirit.

A Note on Sources and Intellectual Debts

I hope the pages of this book fairly reflect some of the insights of contemporary theorizing about the workings of human organizations, complex information processes and political behavior. I have tried very hard to use this body of theory rather than simply to talk about it. The knowledgeable reader will recognize my special indebtedness to a few books with which the novice might well begin. The first are Herbert A. Simon, *Administrative Behavior* (second edition, New York: Macmillan, 1961) and, with James G. March, *Organizations* (New York: Wiley, 1958). Karl W. Deutsch, *The Nerves of Government* (New York: Free Press, 1963) applies the tools developed in the study of communications systems and computers to the entire political structure. A collection of papers edited by Lucian Pye, *Communications and Political Development* (Princeton: Princeton University Press, 1963) summarizes a great deal of the recent work on communications and political change in the so-called, developing countries. Richard L. Meier, *A Communications Theory of Urban Growth* (Cambridge: M.I.T. Press, 1962) suggests the use of time budgets to measure the flow and cost of information. Several propositions raised in this study of New York and only impressionistically validated could be properly tested by systematic calculations of the sort Meier proposes. I look forward to this as a future task. The psychological analysis of social change in Everett Hagen, *On the Theory of Social Change* (Homewood: Dorsey Press, 1962) can, I think, be usefully integrated into this communications approach through the analysis of the transfer of information between generations.

The empirical materials from which this book is fashioned are indicated by and large in the footnotes. I have relied heavily upon government documents, city guides and descriptions, contemporary pamphlets, newspapers, general magazines, trade periodicals and the annual reports of major private organizations. There is relatively little "inside-dope" in this book of the sort which usually delights historians. The major manuscript collection in this field, the Tilden Papers at the New York Public Library, has been shorn of all but a few items of real interest. The Municipal Archives and Record Center of the New York

Public Library houses a great many letters to, from and between city officials. The intense divisions within the city government meant, however, that much of this frequently acrimonious correspondence was released to the press even before it reached the desk of its formal recipients.

Many specialized works about New York history have been helpful in detail but not in general concept. The most important exception to this limitation of local history was Lee Benson, *Merchants, Farmers and Railroads: Railroad Regulation and New York Politics, 1850–1877* (Cambridge: Harvard University Press, 1955). I have learned more from general studies of the process of change in the nineteenth century than I have from local histories. Many readers will detect the strong similarity between the argument of this book and that put forward by David Donald in his essay on "An Excess of Democracy: The American Civil War and the Social Process," *Lincoln Reconsidered* (second edition, New York: Vintage Books, 1961). They may also see that my argument extends and generalizes the treatment of the communications revolution in Richard Hofstadter's *The Age of Reform* (New York: Alfred Knopf, 1955) to the point of suggesting the usefulness of a re-examination of Hofstadter's basic emphasis upon a status revolution as the primary background of progressivism. I benefited from several useful hints on industrial administrative problems in Alfred D. Chandler, Jr., *Strategy and Structure* (Cambridge: Harvard University Press, 1962), Joseph A. Litterer, "Systematic Management; Design for Organizational Recoupling in American Manufacturing Firms," *Business History Review*, XXXVII, 4 (Winter 1963, pp. 369–391), and J. Owen Stalson, *Marketing Life Insurance, Its History in America* (Cambridge: Harvard University Press, 1942).

One final body of evidence—the city itself—requires special mention. The principal survivals of Boss Tweed's New York are not the old buildings but the layout of the streets, building plots, squares and parks. Until 1945 one would not have been far wrong in assuming that whatever one saw had either been designed or accepted into the city plan in the 1860's and 1870's. This assumption is no longer quite so safe. There are fine maps and pictures which help to distinguish old from new in Isaac Newton Phelps Stokes, *The Iconography of Manhattan Island, 1489–1909* (6 vols., New York: R. W. Dodd, 1915–1928) and John A. Kouwenhoven, *The Columbia Historical Portrait of New York* (Garden City: Doubleday, 1953).

INDEX

Printed in the United States
24886LVS00003B/70-126